Becoming Me, Again

Things I Wish I Had Known

Natasha Soregaroli

AOS Publishing, 2024

Copyright © 2024 Natasha Soregaroli

ISBN: 978-1-998662-09-8

Cover Design: Chanelle Poupart

Visit AOS Publishing's website:
www.aospublishing.com

Contents

To the girls who feel alone in their thoughts.

This one's for you.

Introduction

I am writing this introduction as an 18-year-old girl, as I prepare to share thoughts and experiences from my life, from the time I entered my teenage years to the verge of womanhood. It's exactly what I was thinking and feeling at the time that I sat down to write the stories you are about to read.

This is my story of learning to love myself.

This is written based on my experience growing up and my reflections on the things that life has thrown my way.

It is for those who feel alone in their thoughts or are made to feel crazy for thinking them. It's for those who don't feel normal. It's for those who still feel hopeful but, whose hope is usually drowned out by their negative thoughts. It's for people who want a better life, but can't seem to escape the cycle of harsh and harmful thoughts that consume them.

You will be taken on a journey that covers all the things that I encountered along the way as a teenager that confused or frustrated or angered me. I felt lost and there were sooo many things that attacked my self-confidence. I became self-deprecating when it came to my self-image, especially my weight. I searched desperately for that 'Girl Power' I kept hearing so much about, but all I found was the stress and anxiety of social media. I made so many assumptions about myself and my relationships, and, like so many of my peers, I idealized the life portrayed in the movies that I loved watching with my friends. But in the end, I found my way through the dark forest of self-doubt and navigated the jungle of social pressure. I learned how to become me again, how to take control of my life.

I know there is a girl out there who needs this book because this is what I wish I had known when I was experiencing these thoughts. My hope is that it has found you and that it helps you navigate your own journey, that by relating to my experience, you feel NOT alone and that you are NOT going crazy. I hope it inspires you to explore who you are in the world and discover who you want to be.

In full, this is the story of how I dealt with self-confidence issues, self-deprecation, and others' opinions.

I became me, again - you can too.

How To Read This Book

This book is meant to be read with an open mind, and it is not necessarily best to read it in chronological order. I encourage you to read based on titles, sections, and topics that resonate with you.

It is designed to give you the freedom to jump around randomly.

I hope reading about someone else's experience of life will help you feel more understood and seen.

Part 1: I Lost My Way

I was happy and confident in elementary school. I had friends, I played sports, I loved painting, I loved exercising my creativity. But, somewhere along the way, in my teenage years, I lost my way and started to feel alone in my thoughts and the world.

This is how it happened to me...

The Voice Inside Me

I Am Alone in My Thoughts

I spent my childhood in Vancouver, Canada, where I learned to bike, play field hockey, and bake. All life experiences that have guided me to be who I am today. I grew up playing outside in my backyard where I would climb the fig tree.

Even though I had a full life, I was nowhere near fulfilled. It all started when the pressure of the outside world began to consume me. All I knew before the age of twelve was my small bubble: elementary school, sports teams, and family. As my bubble of people began to expand, I found myself listening more to the opinions of others. I took criticism as a personal attack, seeing images plastered on social media as things that I should aspire to replicate, none of which were great for my confidence. By the time I was sixteen, my self-worth had shattered and my understanding of the world had been warped by the constant chatter.

It was a rainy Thursday afternoon. I found myself in my room crying. Again. This time I was crying because my schoolwork was overwhelming.

Or was it because I hated my body?

Or was it because I was fighting with a friend?

Actually, I believe *that* time, like most times, it was all those things compiled into one emotional mess in my brain that amounted to my lungs running out of air, my snotty nose, my bright red eyes, and my puffy face with salty tears streaming downward. But this just seemed to be par for the course in those days. I would cry, then people would support me, and then I would cry again. I had it locked down and it was one of the only things that was consistent in my life at the time.

By staying in this cycle, I had an excuse not to do my work because I had diagnosed myself with depression. I didn't really have depression. Nonetheless, I was so overwhelmed with everything around me, I thought it would be easier to claim I couldn't do anything. This meant that any simple thing I did during the day was therefore an achievement in my mind. The standards to which I held myself collapsed from under me. They were broken and there was no point in saving them. My sense of self was in need of serious and strenuous rebuilding.

High school was hard; everything was too overwhelming. And, once again I found myself bawling my eyes out and on the verge of being done. Completely and utterly done. I wanted to not exist, to fade into oblivion, to run away, to vanish. Something *had* to change, I could not keep living like that anymore. I could not keep blaming the world for everything that had gone wrong in my life. I had to change my perspectives.

I had lost so much of myself that I didn't know what loving myself truly and deeply really felt like. When I had short bursts of happiness, I would hope the feeling would stay, but an hour later that great feeling was gone. These little slices of happiness were nice, but they were definitely not satisfying. It is so easy to believe you are not good enough if you are always looking at others to determine your worth. If you're constantly looking for external validation it can be hard to realize true happiness comes from within. I was so willing to love other people, yet I drew a blank when it came to listing reasons why I might love myself. I lost my self-respect, my self-love, and my self-worth; I was never once told by society that learning to love myself should have been a priority.

I was stuck between a rock and a hard place for most of my teenage years. I scrolled Instagram and felt worse about myself. I bullied myself relentlessly. I listened and believed the voice in my head that said I was *not good enough.*

Not good enough at school.

Not good enough to be deserving of nice friends.

Not good enough to be complimented.

Not good enough at sports.

Just simply. Clearly. Matter-of-factly. Not good enough.

The voice inside of me began to eat away at my self-esteem and that girl's voice guided my feelings of sadness and worthlessness. This voice was a blessing and a curse; maybe she was just trying to protect me from my fears.

My observations of myself were informing her voice. If I saw my stomach sticking out, she would tell me to change my top because you could see a bulge. Listening to this voice in my head drove me to insanity. It felt real at the time, but even though the things she said were lies, I believed her because I had already thought them myself. The voice acted as an emotional barrier that prohibited me from seeing reality. I didn't have to listen to the girl's constant narration in my head, but I chose to. She could say whatever she wanted, and I didn't have to listen, but I did. I chose to listen to her to determine what I could and couldn't do; and I lost myself along the way. The voice knew me so intimately that she knew exactly what to say to feed my insecurity, ultimately making her negative narration so believable.

That voice inside of me felt like something that was dragging me down when it was just trying to protect me from my deepest fears. The voice allowed me to see the benefits and risks to every decision, which enabled me to make informed choices. Over time I had learned to listen to this voice as it helped me rationalize and had proven to be useful. That voice had saved me from acting on intrusive thoughts. It had also saved me from personal embarrassment. Although it had been helpful in the past, it didn't mean that the voice was always correct in its judgment of the current moment.

Even though I knew it was there to help, the voice needed to learn when it was time to stop talking. When I did morning meditation, I really struggled. I closed my eyes, I began to breathe, and listened to the narrative of the meditation, and everything was normal. But when the guide in the meditation said, "relax your body", in my head I would yell "I AM!" I don't think yelling "I AM RELAXED" made me relaxed.

What I couldn't understand is that people marry each other all the time and promise unconditional love to each other. They stand there gazing into each other's eyes and decide to live their life together and be there for each other through thick and thin. They promise to honour each other's limitations, faults, and idiosyncrasies, and they promise to support each other 'until death do us part'. I only realized recently that marriage is about feeling worthy and acknowledging personal strengths and weaknesses. Most people do not make this type of contract with themselves, one where they promise unconditional love. Most people find ways to accept the flaws in others or don't even notice them, but I was my own biggest critic. I found a flaw in myself, and it was the end of the world because it reinforced the thought that I was not perfect and therefore not good enough.

I used to be a really happy kid, but somewhere along the way I had lost myself. A lot of the time, I felt like I didn't know certain things that everyone expected me to, even though they never told me. How was I supposed to know that I would suddenly feel like everyone was judging my every move? I felt alone in my thoughts and thought I was crazy when the reality was that I was having thoughts that were far more common than I realized at the time. I felt like I had no one to talk to and if I did say something, it felt vulnerable and uncomfortable to admit because I never knew if the other person was going to relate or think I was weird.

Part 2: Self-Confidence

Where do I even START???

My awareness of the role I played in the world crept up on me, seemingly out of nowhere. I remember feeling so confident in my friendships. I remember feeling empowered to rise to any challenge that came my way. The world was mine to conquer and enjoy.

Then one day, it wasn't.

I don't know exactly when or how it all changed, but it did. Suddenly, I no longer felt the confidence I once had. I began to second guess my friendships and didn't feel self-assured in my capabilities to conquer the world, let alone be in the world.

What happened?!

These stories are about all of that messy stuff that it just sucks to go through...

Nurture
Your
Environment

I Am Not Confident

I had a habit of looking at other girls and thinking, "wow, she has it figured out," or "I wish I was her."

I did it constantly.

How was I supposed to feel confident when I was constantly comparing myself to others rather than being grateful for what I had? Deep inside I knew I was the only person who could make me feel confident; I mean really, truly confident, not just in moments of happiness.

I thought about the positive aspect of being able to control my confidence, which was that I am the power behind my thoughts. I was the only one responsible for my confidence levels, and they fluctuated all the time. Time and time again, I had given others power over my confidence by letting them have an impact on the way I felt about myself.

This needed to change. More importantly, I wanted to make a change.

This made it hard because as much as I wanted to blame the world around me I knew it wouldn't have helped. I could not blame my parents, teachers, or friends, since it was up to me to improve my mindset. The hard truth was confidence is not found in a vitamin gummy and it is not a predisposed genetic condition. Rather, it must be created and nurtured from within. I had the potential to transform myself into a more confident, happier person by addressing my inner issues.

Due to my fluctuating confidence, some days I felt amazing, and when I did not, I reminded myself that I had felt good in the past so I could get back to that. This was a reminder of a version of myself I knew was achievable.

Sometimes, I would find myself in my room wearing pajama bottoms and a cute top while singing and dancing to loud music blaring from my speakers. Well, at least I did this when my room wasn't a complete mess and there was space on my floor that wasn't covered in clothes. Other times, I would find myself sitting on my bed in a huge, oversized hoodie in the pitch-black, crying while wearing headphones and playing sad songs on repeat. I was polarized when it came to dealing with my emotions and there was definitely no in-between.

My fashion choices, not only in my room, also changed depending on my levels of confidence. I sported a good hat to hide my face, or baggy sweaters to hide my stomach. All of my 'lack of confidence clothes' involved items that hid my insecurities. But wearing baggy clothes made me feel overweight and then I got even sadder... the lesson I learned is that this doesn't work. When I could acknowledge and realize that I felt like I was lacking confidence, I would put on makeup, hoop earrings, then sing energetic songs, and create an environment that would help me regain my footing. Sometimes it helped, sometimes I just had to cry it out first.

I Knew
but
Didn't Believe

It's Not Really About the Cheekbones, is it?

Others probably didn't see the imperfections I saw in myself. I know this because when my friends brought up their so-called imperfections, I had rarely even noticed them before that moment, let alone thought of them as imperfections. To me, these 'imperfections' were things that were a part of what made them who they were, nothing more. Except I used my 'imperfections' to justify and create negative thoughts towards myself.

Were my 'imperfections' really that bad or was it just my perception of them that made me insecure?

If only there were a way to see myself through someone else's eyes but, sadly, there wasn't. Which meant I needed a different approach to feel confident again.

When I was younger, I wished for cheekbones. I begged for cheekbones because I thought they looked stunning on others. By begging, I mean that at night before I went to bed, I would think about my friends' cheekbones and think to myself, "I WANT THOSE". Then I matured a bit and my face changed and eventually got cheekbones, but I didn't like my smile because I thought it looked like I had a double chin. I don't know if I would ever have been happy with how I looked. It wasn't really about the cheekbones, was it?

I also struggled a lot with the appearance of my stomach. Looking at magazines and on social media with featured tall, thin models lowered my self-esteem and made me less comfortable in my body. I knew that models in magazines were not necessarily the most realistic depiction of what women really look like. Models were often edited, had plastic surgery, and wore loads of makeup. I knew that. I didn't want to believe it. I held their appearance as a standard that I should achieve someday, not because I wanted to but because I felt I needed to in order to be accepted and worthy of love. I knew it was unachievable without surgery and I knew it was not good to use these models as a standard of beauty for myself, but that didn't stop me from using it as the basis against which I would judge myself. I couldn't tell you why I did it. I just did.

So ... it was not about whether I had cheekbones or a flat stomach, but rather it was a bigger problem. The problem was I was judging my body based on an ideal that was not even possible. It did not matter what I looked like because, against that standard, I would not be satisfied. I would always be able to find something wrong with myself, no matter what, and that was the problem. I couldn't see it at the time, but my flaws existed only in my mind, and my value wasn't defined by my physical appearance.

I'm Not in Control

Human brains are constantly learning and adapting, and people are able to create and reinforce new self-talk that changes the way we really see ourselves. This change, however, doesn't happen overnight. Our self-talk is like a habit such as biting your nails, running late, complaining, and self-deprecation. They are hard to break because they have persisted for so long and have become part of how we define ourselves.

Confident people carry themselves differently from insecure people. Confident people tend to be decisive and carry their bodies with more power. I knew this from simply experiencing it. When I felt confident, I felt lifted, as if someone was holding a string attached to my head and pulling my shoulder blades back. When I didn't feel so confident, I often felt pushed down, as if I were carrying a weight over my head and shoulders.

Most of the time, when I was in the midst of creating my own confidence, I found that I was faking it. I had to fake it if I didn't believe it because if I didn't, I would never escape the disastrous cycle of self-deprecating thoughts that entangled me. It was so, so, so important for me to believe that I had control over my autonomous thoughts, even if it didn't feel like it. Having this perspective was necessary for my healing. I had to feel in control in order to make the change I wanted to see and experience in the future.

You Have
a Choice

I'm Too Fat to Wear a Two-Piece

When I was a little girl, I routinely wore a bikini, and I didn't think anything of it. I would throw it on, hop in the water, and swim for hours. By the time I became a teenager, I noticed that girls would compare their waist sizes or talk about people's bodies from images on social media. My confidence and comfort around other girls around my age dropped. I became embarrassed to go swimming with my friends because I thought my body was a million times worse than everyone else's. I decided to only wear one-piece swimsuits most of the time because they covered my belly fat. This way I was able to hide my biggest insecurity, yet, in reality, I was bringing more attention to it by having something skintight against it. I actually preferred two-pieces because I loved the styles, but I promised myself that I would never *EVER* show my stomach to the world because it was just too embarrassing. The truth that I hadn't come to realize yet was that no one noticed my body because they were all worried about their own. I discovered this in grade nine when one of my friends wouldn't come swimming because she didn't like her body. The glass bubble of my beliefs in my brain shattered. I wanted to jump on her and yell, "I KNOW! I can relate, too." This was the first time I knew I wasn't alone when it came to hating my body. I knew people made comments about hating their bodies, as teenagers do, but I thought I was the only one who felt uncomfortable and truly believed it. I didn't realize how debilitating these thoughts could become.

By living through this situation, I also realized that I could do something about it. I could make a change. But battling through my emotions and coming to terms with myself had to happen first.

I had chosen to be the girl who wore one-piece bathing suits due to insecurity.

People almost always have a choice when encountering situations that test confidence. You can either curl up into a ball and let the voices in your head beat you down or you can listen to your heart and put on a brave face. I found that I wanted to take the route that allowed me to blame anyone but myself for my situation; I did this a lot. But I realized that I always have a choice. Would I use the power of choice to help myself or beat myself down? My physical body did not determine my worth; however, allowing my body to control my worth reflected who I was becoming. So I chose to make different choices.

I chose to be the girl who wore two-piece bathing suits.

I chose to be the girl who was sporty and athletic.

I chose to be the girl who loved sewing, painting, and creating.

If I could choose to be all those things, then why couldn't I choose to be the happy girl who loved herself and felt confident in her decisions and thoughts?

This Moment Matters So Much

It was April 30th, 2014; my first year at a new school with new friends and I was going to participate as much as I could. My friends had been talking about how fun the track team was, especially when they won medals. Initially, I thought, *I like getting medals, but I don't like running;* and then I thought, *but I want to spend time with my friends and miss school.* So I joined the track team.

I had never been one to race for the sole purpose of crossing the finish line. That's boring, well at least it was for me. It was the day of the track meet, and the track team was loading onto the bus. We were listening to music and singing. Earlier that day, I had asked someone to be my bus partner and I got the aisle seat, which meant that at that moment, life was perfect. We arrived at the field, and I thought, *I can't wait to miss school for a day to be here—all I have to do is run a thirty-second race.* Then the two hundred-meter race was about to begin and I was in one of the first heats, so pretty much everyone was watching. I lined up completely incorrectly because I had no idea what I was doing. If I were honest, I would admit that I cared if I ended up near the bottom of the rankings, because that would be embarrassing. The gun went off and I ran. As I was running, my mind wandered and I was thinking things like, *what a nice day, there are boys on the bleachers, I'm tired.* And then I realized everyone else had finished and I had just passed the halfway point, completely out of breath. The runners behind me were waiting to start, the girls ahead of me had finished, the boys on the bleachers were watching, and I was still running. I shook it off and thought, *I guess the people in my section were fast but I'm sure there will be people who are slower than me.* And I was right that I wasn't the slowest– kind of. This is where people like me tell themselves stories in order to avoid the truth.

I knew my time was bad, but I convinced myself it wasn't because I didn't want to deal with the pain. The list finally came out, and the girls ran to the board where they posted the results and found the sheet that read 'EVENT 9 GIRLS 200 METER DASH Gr 6'. I stood behind a couple of people and waited for the crowd to clear. I started scanning the names from top to bottom. I was looking and looking, and I finally saw my name. I placed fifty-sixth... which wouldn't be so bad if it was out of one hundred or one hundred and fifty. But I came fifty-sixth out of fifty-seven! My first thought was, *this is the day I am going to die.* Then my second thought was, *what are the boys going to think!* And then I thought, *let's hope nobody looks.* So, I went on with my day thinking that this would be the last time I would have to see it, ever. Who keeps grade six race records anyway?

I was not so confident after this, as you probably can imagine. I had to acknowledge that running is not something I care about at all and not something I was willing to put the work into being better at! It is now six years later and, still to this day, I think about that. A couple of years ago, I decided to Google my name, as one does when one is bored or curious, hoping to find something cool or some pictures. I saw this link that read 'Vancouver Elementary Schools R & F Cham 2014'. So I clicked on the link and found my name. It was the sheet that had been posted to the bulletin board four years before. Posted for the whole world to see!!!

Years later, I realized that this event made no difference to my life at all. No difference, except for the small dent in my ego. Experiences like this are a great turning point for people in their lives. Failures can create the person who we are today. When learning to walk, we don't suddenly run a marathon and have perfect coordination, strength, and muscle memory. Rather, we attempt to stand by holding on to something like our parents' fingers or the side of a couch. After a while, our legs collapse under us. Then we learn to put one foot in front of the other, but we only make it a few steps before we fall. This is the process of failing and getting back up again.

It's an important process in life.

As life got more complicated and the failures became a bigger deal to me, I started to forget the importance of getting back up again. When I failed it meant I was trying to accomplish something and pushing myself beyond my limits. A failure allowed me to either persist, pivot, or give up. When I persisted, I kept moving forward and overcame my previous failure. When I pivoted, I chose a different route for something I would rather focus on. And when I gave up, I lost confidence in my abilities and felt sorry for myself. Overcoming failures and problem solving tended to give me a great sense of purpose and positive, self-affirming thoughts.

Ultimately, the 200 Metre Dash event lasted for only a small fraction of my life. It shouldn't have made any difference to the way in which I saw myself, but the reality is that it became one of my most life-defining failures at that time. I think that it probably made no impact on how others saw me, yet my internal value was shattered.

Events like this can feel like such a significant failure, but in the grand scheme of things, they aren't. For me, it was hard to make that distinction at the moment because my emotions took over and gave a false sense of importance to the event. As small or insignificant as it may have been in reality, the way I reacted to the situation definitely impacted how I felt about myself. I have found my post-failure decision-making has the ability to open doors in my life and close the ones I don't care about.

I Need Something Else to Be Beautiful

One warm spring evening I learned that I had magic shoes. Their magic was not the kind that made them appear out of thin air or the kind that teleported me, even though that would have been really cool. It was something better. When I put them on, magic circulated through my body, making me feel like I could accomplish anything. I felt like I was walking the catwalk during Fashion Week in Paris or the red carpet at the Grammys; I always enjoyed imagining that someday I would be up on that stage next to Jennifer Aniston or Robert Downey Jr. When I was out, people commented on my shoes.

In truth, they were out there in terms of colour and funkiness, and they gave the world something to focus on other than my body.

Sulking, hating, and judging was so darn easy that once it became a habit I found it hard to stop. When I was in the midst of not liking myself prior to going out, it wasn't always easy to leave the house feeling so self-conscious. In order to face the outside world and feel better about myself, I had to find something, even if it was small, to help me face the world with confidence.

My shoes brought me to a place of false confidence, which allowed me to focus my energy on something other than myself. I owned a wide variety of shoes ranging from runners to heeled boots, to bright pink and polka dot heels, and surprisingly, I found most of them to be magical. My magic shoes filled a hole when I needed them to, and having something that could fill that hole when I was unable to on my own was so important for my confidence.

My Face is Too Ugly, It Needs Coverage

I used my hair as a curtain to hide my face when I did not feel beautiful. It was a tool I thought could be used to distract the world from myself and I would strategically style my hair to hide my face. Growing up, I became more and more insecure, and unfortunately, these insecurities were sometimes acknowledged by others. The last thing I wanted to know was that others saw me the way I saw me. That's why, when I was seventeen and still finding confidence in my body, a comment from a close family friend was completely confidence-shattering and I still remember her words to this day:

"If only that beautiful hair had a pretty face to go with it"

That comment shook me to my core. It took everything inside of me not to cry in front of her. Not only did that make me even more self-conscious of my face, it also justified my use of my hair as a shield, because at least *that* was beautiful.

I guess I didn't really think about it at the time, but in hindsight, hiding my face damaged my confidence. When I chose to hide my face, it was because I was uncomfortable with who I was and I would do anything to make myself invisible. I felt like covering my face was covering all my self-imposed flaws including my non-existent thigh gap, my belly, and my chubby cheeks. I was not doing anything except isolating myself from the world. When I became aware of its impact, I had two options: I could let myself cave into my insecurities and continue to hide or I could choose to tie my hair up and show my face before it became too scary. The longer that I hid behind my fear the worse it became the more stressful it became, and the more energy I wasted as it became my life's focus.

Accept
the
Compliment

I'm Too Ugly for Someone to Compliment Me

The ability to receive compliments can reflect a person's confidence and ability to accept themselves for who they are.

Up until recently, there were only two ways that I responded to a compliment. For example, if someone said "You are so beautiful" I would respond in one of two ways:

1. "Haha, thanks." I would mutter with my head down and my eyes a little bugged out to show that I didn't really believe it.

OR

2. "Not really, but thank you," I would say, glancing around the room and feeling uncomfortable.

The words "thank you" never came out of my mouth with confidence and self-assuredness or without some kind of negative qualifier. I noticed that if people complimented me on something that I didn't see in myself, I usually felt that it wasn't worth hearing. I couldn't accept the compliments because I had no confidence to start with and I believed that people were lying. I'm pretty sure people knew my secret. They knew I didn't love myself or think I was worthy. Honestly, it was fairly obvious to anyone paying attention.

By rejecting others' compliments, I was not only hurting myself, even if it may have appeared that way. Also, I hadn't even considered the perspective of the person giving the compliment. By rejecting the compliment, I was essentially implying that their opinion was invalid, wrong and that they were lying. None of these were things I wanted someone to feel due to my own insecurity, especially if they were trying to be nice. Accepting a compliment was a really big challenge and sometimes still is. When I could set my mind to really embracing compliments, I began to believe the words others told me. Believing the positive words and affirmations slowly began to increase my sense of self-worth.

I decided to make a change.

It all started as a New Year's resolution. I decided that I would accept every single compliment that was given to me. The first compliment I received tentatively and very awkwardly. Now, I am more inclined to receive compliments by smiling and saying "thank you", yet I still sometimes feel a little embarrassed and awkward. In reality, to some extent, the self-deprecating voice in my head will always be there. Choosing not to listen and deciding to accept compliments was my first step to quieting the negative voices and introducing positive ones.

Ultimately, I realized that I didn't need to believe the compliment in order to accept the compliment. Fake it 'til you make it; it felt uncomfortable and awkward at first, and that's because I was stepping well outside of my comfort zone.

I'm Sorry

When someone held the door for me, a polite thing to say could have been "thank you". But for me, the words 'thank you' were for someone confident. Instead, I would say 'sorry'. When I used to do anything, and I mean pretty much anything, I would apologize. The truth was that I didn't feel worthy of people doing things for me, so I would apologize; I didn't think I deserved it and thought they were wasting their time.

Words are far more powerful than they appear to be. Words are really just words, but they often come with emotions too, and some words have more emotion attached to them than others. The words "I'm sorry" were like that for me. Growing up I was taught to say 'sorry' when responsible for doing something that might be offensive or painful to others. At some point, I noticed that when I said 'I'm sorry', it often made others feel more powerful. As someone who enjoyed the feeling of making others feel good, I didn't mind feeling weak for their benefit, and I didn't think it really mattered if I meant it or not, so I kept saying it. Since I received a lot of positive feedback, I developed a habit of saying it often. But saying "I'm sorry" evoked feelings of guilt within, as if I did something wrong even if this wasn't the case.

It felt like a spell was cast, controlling me with only two small words, "I'm sorry". It was such an insignificant couple of words that it didn't make a difference, right? One shirt on a bedroom floor doesn't make a room messy, while the continuous act of throwing dirty laundry on the bedroom floor accumulates over time. The next thing you know you are dealing with piles of shirts, pants, skirts, dresses, and socks strewn across the room. The clothes consume the room making it almost nonfunctional. The same goes for the repetition of those two words. As the meaning of "I'm sorry" gets reinforced and accumulates, you become more insecure about what you're doing. It works like compound interest. Which is basically a fancy way to say the words we use often have an exponential impact as time passes since the result created from repeating these words is not starting from ground zero. When I continuously said "I'm sorry" the words grew to have more and more meaning and started to take a toll on my self-confidence. Since saying "I'm sorry" implies you are doing something wrong, repeating this when you don't feel a real need to apologize ultimately reinforces that you are never right in your behaviour.

Appreciation for others has a strong connection to self-confidence. This switch from "I'm sorry" to "Thank you" made a huge difference in my life. I suspect when I switched to "thank you" it told the world, not just me, that I was grateful for things in my life. I started to believe that people cared about me which, as a result, made me happier.

I found that thinking about how I used words and switching my vocabulary to an intentional use of words was a way for me to practice self-confidence on a small scale. You may find that you have other words in your vocabulary that act as a form of self-deprecation. With a simple switch, it changed my beliefs and confidence. Most of the time it is the accumulation of little disciplines that have the ability to create greater impact in the future. As the saying goes: There is no such thing as an overnight success. Companies like Apple don't suddenly rise to power in twelve hours. Instead, they work on the projects within their company that will prove they are the best. Every day they work on creating positive customer satisfaction and easy to use products that will enable them to become a success in the future. It's the work they do every day, and although it may seem insignificant at the time, it ends up being the reason they can achieve great things. These little things that Apple does to cater to the user experience increase their value substantially.

The great thing about making changes in vocabulary is that it does not require any superpowers - you just need to be conscious of your words and have a willingness to change automated patterns created over time. I found that it was really about intention and making a conscious effort to use words that empowered me instead of those that made me feel powerless.

I Really Don't Care

Humans have been making decisions since we developed consciousness.

Should I settle down now for the night or wait an hour? Should I go straight or left to avoid a predator?

We are born to make decisions and we have been making decisions since we were babies.

I don't want those mashed peas and potatoes. Should I study for the test tomorrow? Should I eat cereal or toast for breakfast?

We make decisions even when it doesn't feel like we are making them. The act of making decisions is ingrained in our lives whether we like it or not.

When I was in a group setting and there was a decision to be made, especially if I cared about the outcome, I would usually not say anything because I feared picking the thing the other people didn't want. It was all about people-pleasing. I assumed that since I cared about the decision then they did as well.

I also felt like I was being a nuisance or obnoxious for having an opinion, which is probably because I had such an extreme lack of confidence. I didn't think my opinions mattered and were worthy of being heard. I had lost touch with myself and what I cared about because I had disconnected the act of making decisions from being human.

Because I am obstinate, which means that it's very hard for me to change my mind, I found it easier to avoid making decisions as much as possible. The reality was that I struggled, a lot, with changing from one idea to the another, especially when I had a strong opinion about the first idea.

The hardest part about being decisive is remembering to be flexible with what is going to happen in the future in order to be happier with any outcome. Therefore, if I didn't mentally anchor and prepare myself based on a decision to begin with, then I was not stuck on an idea of what I really wanted so I would be happy if plans changed. Essentially it was about my ability to manage my expectations.

By learning to make decisions and also be flexible with my expectations, I discovered that it is sometimes even better if things don't always go according to the plan in your head.

I Think That, Too

"Same!"
"Yes, I can relate."
"Me, too!"

Sometimes I liked feeling like I could relate to things even when I didn't share that experience. Realistically, my own experiences are all I know. So even when I heard someone say something like "I've gained so much weight", whether or not it was true, my immediate reaction tended to be, "same!". Agreeing with others and finding common ground, rather than being true to myself, felt like the easiest way to fit in.

I wanted to belong.

I wanted to find my people.

More importantly, I wanted people to like me.

Fitting in and feeling like part of a community was so important for me to feel good about myself.

Sometimes the peer pressure to fit in was strong enough for me to disregard my own values and act differently. You may even find that the biggest risks you take are not when you are by yourself. For some reason, being in a group and watching others do what you know you shouldn't, can feel like a justification for your actions. You most likely don't drink in your bedroom by yourself, yet you might be more inclined to drink with your friends.

By learning to pause and think about how I truly felt, rather than automatically agreeing with someone, I became more of my own person rather than just trying to fit in with the status quo. My identity no longer felt attached to those around me when I stopped just trying to make others happy. I was able to listen to my friends and understand what they were going through without trying to relate. By detaching from the "follow the leader" mentality, I allowed myself to become the person I wanted to be. If I went against what my friends were doing, it didn't mean that doing this was bad, it just meant that others were making different decisions from myself. Their choices were not my choices. You are your own person. It was important for me to realize this when interacting with others so I continued to be my own person instead of succumbing to my initial instinct of mindlessly agreeing with others.

I believe the saying 'show me your friends and I will tell you who you are' is true. That's why the thing that helped me the most was distancing myself from the people who didn't help me become the person I wanted to be. I lost quite a few friends when I did this, although "friends" might be a loose term. More than anything, I didn't want their negative influence in my life. I created a small bubble of friends who I knew would support me. This bubble was very small. Tiny. To this day, I have three close friends, and they are incredible, supportive, and inspiring.

I found that many things came out of my mouth that didn't speak to who I was just because of the influence that my friends were having on me. I was hanging out with them so much that they became the standard for what was becoming a new normal for me. My normal was, still is, defined by who I surround myself with. Friends influence your thoughts and behaviours and shape who you become. Knowing this also allowed me to make the changes I needed to make in order to become who I wanted to be.

Keeping
Busy

I Look Gross in That Picture

I really struggled when looking at pictures of myself and would always criticize my body instead of thinking, "Wow, I am beautiful". Unfortunately, I believe this is common for many other girls and women, especially when taking pictures for Instagram. In groups, I often heard my peers say, "You can't post that one, I look bad. What about this one?" and then another one replies, "No! I look bad in that one. Let's just take another one." Sure, it makes sense and I completely understand, but when did society become so shallow? When did our looks become so important?

Was it due to the influential fashion industry that changed the way we see beauty? Was it your idea of perfection ultimately rubbing off on others? Was it boredom? Are these thoughts of not being good enough ingrained in our bodies and DNA?

As a teenager, my hormones became, or at least felt much more intense. Having to adjust to so many changes and influences - my period, a new body and new relationships - made it really hard for me to remember who I was at my core.

So... was the picture that important? When did I start criticizing the pictures of me? How do I stop believing a bad picture of myself reflects my value?

I know that being productive helped my confidence. During the last few years of high school, it was easier to keep busy with work, sports, friendships, and academics. These consumed time, decreasing my encounters with boredom so I had no time to worry about what I looked like. Activities gave my life focus when I needed a distraction from who I was. The more I thought about my future, the more confused I became; however, the more I focused on living in the moment, the more accomplished I felt. Focusing on the end goal just overwhelmed me instead of inspiring me to take the steps to get there. I'm not saying that filling your life with activity can be the way to not feel self-conscious or sad, but having activities allowed me to think about other things. And my thoughts tended to be very depressing when I sat alone for too long. I started to compare myself to everyone and everything else because it was my only way of making sense of the world and who I was in it. By doing things, it was a perfect distraction from thoughts that didn't necessarily add to my life. I think it is so important to play, try new things, and work when you're young. This allowed me to gain new perspectives of the world around me because I had so much experience trying new things. Whether that be working as a cashier, playing field hockey, or writing in a journal.

Part 3: Self-Deprecation

Why didn't anyone tell me that your friends change as you get older? That *you* change. That *everything* changes.

That you like different things.

That you want different things.

That you'll start to second guess everything you once knew.

That you'll feel worse about yourself with no real explanation as to why.

This is how my self-deprecating thoughts influenced my life and how I learned to deal with them...

Avoidance

I Hate the Mirror, and the Mirror Hates Me

Looking felt like walking alone in a dark alleyway.
It felt like a bullet grazing the scar layered skin of her left
arm.
It felt like standing alone speechless, swallowed by a stage.

Her thoughts stood manipulated by social trends and
expectations.
The stress of others' opinions pumped through her veins
aggressively.
All her decisions influenced by her elixir
Of surrounding screens and papers in newsstands.

She stood looking in a mirror
With its old rusty silver film and waterproof paint slathered
on.
Looking felt like an undiagnosed virus, rare and odd.
She noticed the case of the mirror was a shiny gold with an
intricate pattern.
Even the mirror was beautiful.

Her body dried out like an internal desert.
She waited for her rain, her fuel, to shower her desert.
Waiting for the rain felt like a metal sword cutting into her
skin.
The sword in a parasite's custody,
Splitting skin causing pain-infused words to spill out,
Spilling like clumped red blood oozing out of a wound.

The mirror can become such a scary place growing up, at least it was for me. It was an opportunity to criticize myself. It allowed me to see what others see, and be ruthless. I found that I was often unrecognizable. I felt a certain way, but looking in the mirror I didn't look the way I felt; there was a disconnect. Was I gaslighting myself into thinking I looked different than I did because I didn't want to believe the reality? Was I seeing clearly?

All I knew was that as soon as I looked in the mirror I felt disgust. Oof that was a hard pill to swallow. Standing in front of the mirror, intimately nitpicking my features, one by one, until nothing was left, was not that abnormal for me growing up.

This was not the purpose of a mirror, was it?

I Can't Stand the Way I Look

A long time ago, I never, ever would have thought I'd find myself staring in my mirror and repeating the words, "I am beautiful and confident".

The mirror in my bedroom changed around the age of twelve. It developed a sassy personality and became really mean. Instead of being a mirror that allowed me to check if I had food in my teeth or dirt on my face, it developed a new purpose. The mirror became a place where I looked to judge myself. I thought it had become a safe space where I could put myself down without others noticing; never did I think my thoughts would be reflected through my behaviour and how I carried myself in the world. I was unconsciously brainwashing myself to feel unworthy and my mental health went downhill from there. Every time after that when I found myself in front of the mirror saying something unkind, I would make a strong effort to switch what I was saying into, "I am beautiful and confident" while staring deeply into my own eyes. When saying it, I learned to feel and believe the words with my whole body. I realized that sometimes it's not about believing the words before saying them that matters, but rather saying the words you want to believe until you really start to believe them.

I Look Horrible in Pictures

It was a warm day in June and the sun shone through the large windows of our living room. The grass was greener than ever and there was not a cloud in the sky. You know when things are going too well, and it feels hard to be happy? That was how I felt. I was waiting for that slap in the face that would turn my world right back to how it always was—sad and emotional.

My field hockey photo had just arrived, and I was bouncing off the walls, excited to see it. The package was concealed in a bag, so I opened it up with joy and positivity beaming from my eyes. I had always loved field hockey because it gave me a place where I could release my energy and competitiveness. I ripped the package open and pulled out the photo. I was stunned. My first thought was, *What!? I'm not even in it!* And then my second was, *who is that short six-year-old at the end?!* I realized that 'short six-year-old' was me. I was the girl sitting at the end, a foot shorter than anyone else in the photo.

What really upset me was that I was not even the shortest player on our team! I was the *second* shortest! And to some short people, like me, that's a BIG difference. I hadn't realized until that moment that I had such a tiny torso, and I didn't like it. From that point on I made a promise to myself that *I would never EVER sit in a photo again!* And, as much as it is humanly possible, I have kept that promise to myself ever since.

The truth was I wasn't ashamed that I was short, because by that point in my life, I had come to accept it, but it was the thought that others might think that being small made me weak. People tend to become what others perceive them to be, which is why I believed the lies I told myself. It felt like the message was being reinforced by others. These lies were only the stories I made up in my head because when you don't have all the information, you do what everyone else does. You fill in the blanks.

From a young age, we are programmed to fill in the blanks and make assumptions. These assumptions are stories that you make up in the absence of fact, and they are more like realistic fairy tales. This programming makes things seem obvious in certain situations without us having to be told.

If I'm really honest, I can say that I'm traumatized by the kids on the playground who used to point at the scar on my face and yell, "EWWWW". But, in spite of all that, I was by far my own biggest bully... because I chose to listen and believe that I wasn't good enough. Once I had this belief, I formed ideas and thoughts to feed the illusion and justify the false story that was in my mind and my heart.

If you're wondering what kinds of thoughts these were, these are the types of things I said to bully myself into feeling worse because I was insecure:

I'm not good enough. I look like a boy. I have a mustache. Girls hate me. I have no friends. I feel alone. My legs are too big. No one will love me. My arm fat is embarrassing. I want to look like her. I have a unibrow. My stomach is too big. I'm ashamed to go out in public. My acne is disgusting. No one will like my scars. I hate myself. I'm ashamed of who I am. My face is chubby. I look too young. My torso is too short. I have to change myself to be loved. Boys won't like me back. My hair is too short/long. I'm too thin/fat. My boobs are too small/big. My cheekbones are so fat. I'm stupid/dumb. My eyes aren't pretty enough. My butt is too small/big. My body is too hairy. My life is a mess. I am useless. I'm uglier than all my friends. My eyes are too small/big. I already have wrinkles! I'm inadequate. I have to hide my body. My hands are too chubby.

Just because I had these thoughts didn't mean that they were true and it doesn't mean I think them now. My past does not define who I am and who I choose to be right now in the present. What a way to live, constantly worrying about my physical appearance and what others might think. Surprisingly, this did not make me happy.

Shocking, *I know*!!!

All that being said, these thoughts were fleeting if I allowed them to be. If I hung onto them to establish my value and self worth then that was a choice I made which contributed to the way I defined my identity and portrayed myself in the world.

I Need To Be Perfect

Have you ever tried looking at yourself in the mirror and intentionally saying positive things?

Probably not.

But have you looked in a mirror or a reflection in a window when you walked by and thought, "ewww..." I have. I honestly did it daily because I couldn't help it. And do you know what I began to realize?

It was a bad habit.

Habits are a blessing and a curse. I have found that they either helped me or hurt me. That's why it was so important for me to foster an environment that supported good habits. Habits can be hard to break, and yet, they can be created fairly easily. My definition of a habit is something very simple that you do daily or often, like brushing your teeth twice a day or always clicking snooze when your alarm goes off in the morning (some habits are good, and some are bad).

I had a habit of putting myself down and I don't think I'm alone in this. This bad habit impacted me in more than just one way. I was unable to accept compliments, and I constantly talked negatively about myself, so I never had a period of relief where I felt good about who I was.

I also had lots of perfectionist tendencies, and in some ways, I still do, because I was never EVER satisfied with my results for anything. For example, a high score on a test didn't feel good enough, my fashion sense was never as good as others, and my writing was never neat enough. The list could probably go on forever, which just added to the list of reasons that justified my self-deprecation. My expectations for myself were way too high and I came to that conclusion by planning out what my perfect life would actually look like. The list is written below; remember that all these things are on top of an eight-hour work or school day and homework:

- *Meditate (twenty minutes)*
- *At least thirty minutes of exercise / ten thousand steps a day*
- *Practice visualization (one hour)*
- *State self-affirmations*
- *Wake up naturally*
- *Chores (laundry, cleaning)*
- *Nine hours of sleep*
- *Healthy meals (breakfast, lunch, dinner)*
- *No sugar, no dairy, no gluten, no alcohol*
- *List out your top five priorities of the day*
- *Plan your day tomorrow*
- *Drink eight cups of water*
- *Don't touch technology an hour before you go to bed*
- *Early mornings (half past five to six am)*
- *Take at least thirty minutes for lunch*
- *Journal (twenty minutes)*
- *At least thirty minutes reading*

- *Clean room*
- *Socialize (family & friends)*
- *Cute outfits and makeup*
- *Time for self-care*
- *Skin care routine*
- *Shower*
- *Gratitude thoughts*
- *Little to no use of technology*
- *Side hustle*

WHERE DO I START?

I finally realized the stupidity of it all. If I were to do everything people told me I should do, and everything I wanted to do in a day, I'd barely skim the surface of completing them, because there are an unlimited number of things you can do for yourself to make your life better.

I decided to narrow down the things that meant the most to me, because looking at that long list was too overwhelming. So, I chose two to three, other than necessities like showers and eating. Another frame of reference that helped me was to choose things that are very important for mental health, so wearing cute clothes is not a number one priority to me. Even though it may boost my confidence, it doesn't have to be a daily practice.

I often found inspiration in a moment, and although I had good intentions and set reasonable goals, it was common for me to lose interest in a couple of days and then give up. I was bad at sticking to it. It was hard to maintain my motivation. It felt like I was fighting with myself, and I wonder if it was because I had a deep inner fear of leaving my comfort zone and changing who I was. At least I knew the person I had become - she was familiar and I knew what to expect, even if I didn't like being her all that much.

I would often create a goal for myself, then create ways to cheat the system, which was really just cheating myself. When I cheated myself, it made me feel less accomplished because I knew deep down that it wasn't aligned with my values. I used to think, *well, when I was driving, I read the McDonald's sign and street names so that should count as my daily reading,* but at the end of the day, I was only cheating myself. No one else was going to hold me accountable for my actions. There is a saying that goes 'you need to put in the work to see the results', and this system kind of works for me. I was expecting the results to appear out of thin air without much work, but unfortunately, those results never appeared.

My self-deprecating thoughts were the standards I created for myself. When I thought negative things about myself and said them out loud, my actions tended to be a reflection of these thoughts. Saying them out loud would also give people around me validation to put me down because I didn't believe I deserved more. I encountered this a lot when I made self-deprecating jokes - people would laugh and treat me differently. They would treat me like I wasn't worth their time, and I began to lose friends.

In terms of constantly seeking perfection, I felt like the standards I had set for myself were unattainable by someone like me.

Someone like me? Someone who feels like they aren't good enough. Someone who feels unworthy. Someone who feels like a victim of today's advertisements

I Hate Myself and I'm So Unhappy

A lot of the time I would focus on the superficial things in life, like my dry skin, my scars, my weight, and my voice that sometimes cracked. Yet my bigger concerns went below the surface. All of my physical appearance concerns seemed to lead to the same underlying issue: am I good enough? I knew deep down that it wasn't about whether my dry skin would give me wrinkles or shaving my legs would help me be accepted by society, and yet, it was social pressures that drove me to make decisions that I thought would make me good enough. I was wrong. No matter what I did, I was never good enough. Eventually, I learned to appreciate what I already had. I stopped wanting what others had and gave up trying to chase perfection that didn't exist.

Personal reflection was essential for me to really understand myself. I had to face myself even if I didn't like what I saw.

I thought a lot. About random stuff. I was an overthinker, and still sort of am. Thinking things through is part of who I am, and I especially like to think things through on my own.

It took two years for me to decide whether I wanted to shave the upper part of my legs. I felt the pressure from other girls, and in hindsight, I realized women tend to pressure you about things they are self-conscious about themselves. My mother helped me see reality by talking to me openly about the use of Photoshop on women online. She once said to me, "next time you are walking on the street, look for a woman who looks like someone straight out of a magazine, and there will be none." This made sense in my mind, but the truth was that I didn't really believe it. I tried it for a while, and after the third day, I realized that what she said was in fact true. Of course, there were beautiful women on the street, but there weren't 'fake' women. What happened to the women with big lips, thin waists, and big breasts? Did they disappear overnight? I came to the conclusion that they were never there to start with, but that didn't stop me from using them as my standard of ideal beauty.

Cameras have filters on them that alter certain aspects of what comes through in a photograph. My eyes had a filter for my life that only allowed me to see what would justify my thinking and beliefs. In other words, since I believed that women in magazines were beautiful with their alterations, inevitably I felt like I wasn't good enough because I didn't have plastic surgery to look like them. I blurred out the real world in front of my eyes because it wouldn't prove my point that all women were perfect except for me. What was stopping me from changing the lens over my eyes to help me internalize different messaging, like photographers who change their camera lens to capture new images of the same landscape or object?

I've rocked many hairstyles, including one when I was eight years old that made me incredibly self-conscious. Instead of focusing on the length of my hair, I decided to focus on the glimmer of hope in my eyes and the fire in my soul.

I have donated my hair to cancer four times, and I didn't donate it because I thought I would look smoking hot in my new, short, frizzy bob. I donated because I loved the way I felt when I was giving something precious of mine to someone who needed it more. This ability to give something of mine gave me a sense of pride and the external validation that I craved and needed at the time.

Honestly, I didn't think I would like who I was if I spent any time thinking about myself. I remember the time when I stood in the kitchen for an hour bawling so much that my vision clouded. I remember the time when I lay under a blanket, choking on my tears and holding my breath, hoping that I would fade away and eventually run out of air. I remember the collapse I felt in my chest after this happened and my mom found me. We sat on the couch and she held me in her arms for hours as I cried. It wasn't one thing that had put me over the edge, it was many things combined, like thoughts about not being good enough and the stress of letting others down. I guess life isn't supposed to be happy all the time. Maybe I wouldn't have been able to appreciate life as much if it hadn't been for self-deprecating thoughts strangling my brain. Just because I felt like I wanted the world to end didn't mean that I was depressed or anxious.

In fact, this made me human.

When these self-deprecating thoughts became overwhelming and uncontrollable, I needed strategies to cut off their influence. What I saw from these experiences was hope. I learned the importance of the power of control and how to regain control once lost. I learned to create new confidence boosting thoughts, instead of letting self-deprecating ones swallow me up and guide me to dark places. In order to do this, I had to learn to stop myself from thinking freely and going down a rabbit hole, if it was even possible.

I Am
Beautiful
and
Confident

I Deserve To Be Called Ugly

When I was 17, I was in Italy on a bus and was writing in my journal, just thinking about life. I had imagined being in Italy and travelling the world for so long; it was one of the most amazing trips of my life. I felt so grateful at that moment to have the opportunity to do this. Of course, while I was in one of the most spectacular places in the world, I decided to think about something that had been really bothering me.

My thoughts were overwhelmingly focused on wishing that no one else would have to deal with me, even though I knew that was pretty much impossible. As long as I was living, people would have to deal with me. They would have to deal with my talking about topics they might not find interesting. They would have to deal with my crying when I was sad. Anything that made me remotely human and normal felt like I was a major inconvenience to others.

I came to understand that it was all about perception. Why hadn't I realized that insulting myself was as bad as insulting someone else? If I could use this perspective to detach myself from the image I had of myself, I could potentially see what others saw. That is when I decided that I wanted an identical twin because calling her ugly would be insulting and I would finally understand that calling myself ugly would be no different. I looked towards this idea when I needed a crutch to help myself realize that I am worthy. For some reason, I struggled to extend the kindness I had for others to myself. By thinking about myself as another human, I became more aware of how I talked to myself. It helped me change my mindset and deal with my self-deprecating thoughts that I was worse than everyone else and therefore I wasn't good enough.

I found that I would say negative things to myself throughout the day which ultimately led me to feel useless and like I should just give up on everything. I found myself saying, *"my life is falling apart"* and when looking at others I thought, *"they have the perfect life"*. Or I found myself saying, *"I don't like my body, especially not my stomach rolls and I have face fat."* But when looking at others I thought, *"she has the perfect body and perfect life, and that bathing suit fits her so well"*.

At the end of the day, it felt like I knew too much about my own life to fantasize and romanticize it and I didn't know much about the lives of others so I could romanticize their lives. Of course, others' lives can seem more appealing because you don't usually know their struggles. You have no idea what others are going through, but you know exactly what you're going through. You consume information through a filter, as does everyone. This filter can create the illusion that someone else's life is ten times better than yours because you don't see the whole picture of their life.

You may know what it's like to encounter failure and feel like you're not good enough. You know what your own life feels like, in every possible way. Imagine basing all your feelings about your life on only one encounter with yourself.

How do you think that might change your perspective?

Try to think of one experience or situation in your life that represents who you are as a whole. You probably can't. All the things that have happened in your life cannot be summed up by one tiny percentage of your life. Except that's what you try to do with others.

Like most people, I have experienced things that people would not assume at first glance. I've had shingles, my grandfather has passed away, I've struggled with my weight, and I've had crutches six times. You haven't lived my life, and I haven't lived yours.

I shouldn't call myself anything I wouldn't call anyone else because, essentially, that is a form of bullying. Bullying myself made me less happy, and ultimately, meaner to people around me. This all comes back to dealing with the root of the problem, and the roots were my self-deprecating thoughts.

Accepting and respecting yourself is so important in becoming your true self and knowing your worth.

I Can't Do This

Sadness is like a ball rolling down a hill; it has a crazy momentum where it just keeps going. To switch its direction, you have to get in front of it, stop it, and start pushing it up the hill in the other direction. But the ball still wants to go down the hill. Why? Well, because of gravity. It's being pulled down. Just like the ball rolling down a hill, it is much easier to be sad and make excuses about being sad than to make a genuine effort to change and do something about it.

It is hard to change the momentum of our thoughts.

I quit the gym before even fully committing because it was too hard, not because it was physically challenging, but because there was emotional friction standing in my way. The first time I went to the gym alone I started crying. I didn't want to go because my previous patterns of not going were easier for me. I allowed the momentum to take over and I missed one day, then two, then two hundred.

It is easy to skip the gym. It is easy to buy lunch every day. It is easy to sleep in. It is easy to be sad.

It is harder to go to the gym. It is harder to make your own lunch. It is harder to wake up early. It is harder to be happy.

Yet when you can find a reason that holds you accountable to doing something, it seems easier. You may find it easier to wake up if you are planning to have an early meeting.

You might go to the gym if you listen to music or go with a friend. You may find it easier to be happy once you find techniques to do so. It isn't about finding it hard or easy, but rather, it is about making it easier to do the things you want to do.

It's about forcing functions... things that force you to do something. Make it harder not to stick to your goals than to stick to them.

When I was feeling down, it would have been so easy to turn on sad music and cry, and honestly, I did that sometimes. But when I needed to feel better, I couldn't be doing this. When I had unkind thoughts about myself that made me sad, I turned on loud songs with positive lyrics to drown out the voices in my head. I did this because I was trying to let the words in the songs replace my own voice and compliment me without realizing it. When I said the words from songs out loud, I found that I actually believed them if I said them often enough. I believe it has something to do with tricking my brain into believing something even when I don't.

Be A
Main
Character

My Physical Features Define Who I Am

I know what it's like to have someone stare at your face and I know what it's like to feel uncomfortable showing your face. Due to a scar on my face, I have experienced being stared at, and it is not the most loving or welcoming of feelings. Additionally, instead of acne, I had really dry skin, which actually increases wrinkles, so I was very self-conscious of that growing up. Another thing that people weren't aware of was that I had acne on my chest, and because I was ashamed, I would only wear the types of clothes that covered it. Even though people couldn't see my insecurities, it didn't mean they weren't there.

During my years in high school, there was a lot of talk about acne. Whenever people talked about it and I tried to join in on the conversation, some people would say, "Shut up! You have perfect skin!" What people failed to see was that just because my skin didn't show acne on my face very often, it didn't mean my skin was 'perfect'. In fact, my skin was far from perfect; I have a big scar on my chin, acne on my chest, and red bumps along the sides of my arms. But maybe it wasn't about me. Maybe I didn't need to join in the conversation.

One of my biggest challenges, but greatest moments of awareness, was taking a step back and realizing that I didn't know what happens in other people's lives. Another big realization for me was that people are generally self-centered. Many people need to feel heard, seen, and unique, which means that if you bring something up that distracts the topic from them or makes them feel like they aren't the only one that suffers, they feel unheard and hurt, and want to draw the attention back to them.

I like to feel important, and I believe others do, too, but this means that it can be very easy to resort to unconscious narcissistic behaviour. I define unconscious narcissism as the act of attempting to bring attention to yourself and always suggesting "I" in a statement. For example, if someone states, "my parents got mad at me last night" this person tends to want sympathy and curiosity; however, an unconscious narcissist would say something like, "I remember when my parents yelled at me because I went to a friend's house without asking." This obviously re-directs the conversation and changes the focus. Most people do this a lot without realizing it. It is so easy to believe that my problems are worse than others' problems and compare issues in order to feel important. And it's true - my issues can often seem worse than yours because they are mine and they feel worse to me. Your issues are likely to feel worse to you because they are yours. My problems are never as important to someone else as they are to me, so if I wanted to see change, I would have to create it within myself.

I realized that the girls who accept and are confident with their visible physical differences, like acne or scars, are still attractive. I learned that when it comes to physical appearances, people are rarely satisfied with what they have. So I decided to appreciate what I have instead of wanting what others have or craving perfection that doesn't exist.

You may find that you are quite self-conscious about something on your face, but the truth is that the things that make you insecure don't define who you are. They are not an imperfection, but rather what makes you, you. You may notice that you, too, guide the conversation to yourself without noticing it or you may notice how it feels when someone does this to you.

The biggest key to change is becoming aware and noticing the changes that can be made. And it is important to keep in mind that no one else will find what you perceive as "imperfections" as traumatizing as you do. The good thing about people having a need to feel important is that they are constantly distracted by their own problems. Other people have insecurities, too, so even though you may be thinking that people are staring at your face, they are probably just self-conscious about their own arm fat, big nose, or left eye being smaller than their right.

Unfortunately (or fortunately!), you are not that important in most people's minds. Sooooo let's have our main character moments because we are the main character in our own story and the secondary character in other people's stories.

Part 4: Weight

Weight. When did this EVER matter?

It doesn't. It didn't. And then it did.

These are the stories of when I let weight dictate my self-worth...

My Number On The Scale Matters

I stood in my bathroom on a sacred metal square that read numbers out loud to me. I was a number.

My number: 130 pounds.

What? 130 pounds! How? 130 POUNDS! No way. My friends cried at the idea of being above 110 lbs. This couldn't be right. Except that it was, and that made it official - I was fat. 130 pounds?! I was embarrassed.

It's what mattered most. Nothing else mattered at that moment. The number displayed on the scale below me was me. The number was locked safely away, privately, in that room, but it haunted me and followed me everywhere.

The number never used to be that big. You know, before, when that number was great when I was 11 years old. Why couldn't it have stayed at that?

The number changing wasn't the issue, it was me. I was the one making it an issue. No one else noticed my changing number because no one else cared.

Most girls know their number. It's an identifier. Isn't it?

If girls ask about your number, the lower the better. But boys and men would never ask, at least they shouldn't. But girls think they care about the number. I noticed every changing number, even if it was only by a decimal place. I assumed others did as well. But my number was hidden in one room only.

A few months went by, and my number dropped. I felt good and I knew others noticed. But then, it started to rise again. My number kept changing. Always changing.

AAAHhhh I wanted to scream, so frustrating! The number was a curse. I preferred not to know it but I couldn't help it. People say ignorance is bliss, but it felt like torture. This number was essential to living. Without it, I lost complete control.

When the number rose, I starved myself. When it fell, I indulged. There was no balance. It was an unbreakable cycle.

It was just a number, but it was powerful. It controlled my habits, my attitude, my confidence, and my thoughts. My happiness changed based on the fluctuating number I saw engraved on my soul.

I didn't want to talk about my number, but at the same time, it consumed me. Talking about it was the only way to get it out of my system. It was a grey area because if I complained or expressed how I felt, others would say I was fishing for compliments, or they would say my number wasn't that big. But my number always felt bigger than most.

When I walked into school with my eyes down and others stared at me, I thought they knew my number. People stared in the changing rooms, too, which is why bathroom stalls acted as my second home right before swimming. My number made me insecure and that's why it was secured behind closed doors.

My feet stood firmly on the ground as though being forced down by a heavier weight, like the stress of something you've been meaning to do for days but have been putting off. I heaved my feet up onto the scale one more time, praying my number had changed for the better. But my weight stayed the same.

Tears streamed down my face as I stood alone with the door closed, the world shut out from my number. I prayed that no one would notice. I didn't say "weight" because it was a trigger word. It came with sad thoughts.

I felt lightheaded as I stared into nothingness. I was entranced with myself in the mirror as my number clouded my vision. My reflection was murky.

This number wasn't me. I knew that. I didn't believe it.

My Weight Matters

I thought the number on the scale, and the fat on my stomach defined who I was and determined my likability. I felt like people would treat me differently based on my weight, even if it changed by a few pounds here and there.

I was very aware of my weight, which resulted in the unhealthy relationship I had with it. By this, I mean I struggled with feeling overweight, even when I was not, which ended up lowering my confidence.

You may have looked at a picture of me and thought, "she can't seriously feel fat". I was aware that I was not obese or plus size, but that did not mean that I did not feel like I was sometimes. I felt at odds with myself because my self perception was something that I knew wasn't true.

I constantly looked at myself and said, "am I good enough? Thin enough? Curvy enough…" I found it really hard to look at myself with an unbiased view, especially when I was feeling down. It was an ongoing cycle of feeling great and feeling like I was being weighed down.

The best and worst thing about weight is that it fluctuates. In the morning, I looked in the mirror and saw a model in a *Vogue* magazine, but by the time I got home at night, I saw a naked mole rat. Sometimes I would ease up on myself and think of myself as more of a couch potato. These descriptions of myself were not exactly designed to boost my confidence, but to be fair, in those moments I did not want to.

You may find yourself in a cycle similar to the one that I often got caught up in. It was the cycle of feeling confident with my weight and then wanting to be twenty pounds skinnier or heavier. For me, I always felt a little chubby, but I was aware that many girls felt too skinny. You might find that the cycle you experience causes a weight-focused life. When I had a weight-focused life, it was probably the unhappiest I had ever been. If you have a weight-focused life, then maybe it is time to set weight aside and focus on other goals. I found that by focusing solely on weight it caused severe stress around this topic and usually caused more weight gain. So, instead of saying my goal is to lose fifteen pounds, it was important to phrase the sentence differently, such as my goal is to go to the gym for forty-five minutes at four pm, four days a week. The goal is to create a habit for a healthier lifestyle that focuses on more than physical appearance.

Sometimes I felt good in my skin. Most of the time I wanted to escape it. I didn't know if it is because of the generation I have grown up in, where social media and the perfect image of models are plastered everywhere in the world. Or if it was the constant obsession with myself and the need to dissect every aspect of my face in order to determine my worth. Snapchat and Instagram were no help in breaking that cycle. They displayed a constant stream of content that pictured thin celebrities and influencers which reinforced my inner dialogue that I was too fat.

Weight is something I have always felt self-conscious about. If you feel the same way, then you know what it's like to be obsessed with everything physical about yourself. I saw my cheeks as fat, or my thighs as too big, or my stomach that wasn't flat enough. I know this feeling of breaking down every part of your body and saying negative things because it's easier to criticize than compliment. But when I did this, when I put myself down, the only person I was hurting was myself. Because I was creating a version of myself that was inaccurate.

Say, for example, you become very dependent on the superficial features of yourself, and others, but then your physical appearance changes due to something that is out of your control, such as a car accident. If someone only likes you because of who you were on the outside, chances are your relationship will not last after that.

Physical appearances change, but your mind and heart remain constant. Focus on creating a beautiful person on the inside and you will be seen as beautiful on the outside. You are born with unique differentiators that make you who you are. No matter how different you are, there are over seven billion people on this earth, so chances are many people will love you for being different. It is easier said than done, but once you have learned to embrace yourself, and I mean really, truly learned, then happiness will flow to you in all directions.

I Am Fat

I remember looking at the girls with flat stomachs and thinking I was fat. It was worse at the swimming pool during the summer or in the dressing room at school. There were girls with flat stomachs everywhere, or at least that's how it seemed. But then, who knows? Maybe I was only seeing what I wanted to see.

In myself, I saw fat and I felt fat, and that made it official. I was fat. But I was not actually fat. My stomach tucked in near the belly button and filled out at the hips.

In reality, it wasn't about my weight. No matter how much my mom told me I was a normal weight, I shook it off and thought she was only trying to make me feel better. I convinced myself that the people telling me I wasn't overweight were lying. I became very skeptical of the people around me and lost trust in them. My struggle with weight impacted me more mentally and socially than anything.

You may already be aware that all bodies look different, and they're not only classified into two categories. There is more than just fat and skinny. The biggest thing is to be happy with what you have because if you are not happy with what you have, you probably never will be.

There is something within you that craves things that others have. For the longest time, I wanted other people's chins because they were not scarred, and I realized that so many people took this for granted. I used to go looking at other people's perfect chins because it was something that I didn't have, but it ultimately made me feel worse. I needed to stop focusing on what I didn't have because it was a pointless way of making myself feel worse.

See yourself as fit and healthy. See yourself as beautiful and happy. See yourself for what you have and who you want to be.

Feeling
Worthy

All I Want to Do Is Lose Weight

At around the age of seventeen, I realized when I weighed over a certain amount, I stopped loving myself. Up until then, it had been a constant game of testing the limits of how much I could eat without gaining a substantial amount of weight. I treated the scale like a sacred tablet that told me my worth. Even though I saw models of empowered women who were all shapes and sizes, I never understood how they could feel so comfortable in their own skin. So instead of focusing on losing weight, I decided to shift my target to learning to love myself.

You may find that you have self-imposed limits on yourself as well. These barriers hold your mind at a certain focus, and it may feel like it's hard to escape this cycle of thought.

When I became a teenager and more aware of standards and society's expectations, the way I behaved in society changed. Surprisingly, one of the unfortunate changes in behaviour involved my eating patterns. I was comfortable eating whatever, and whenever, when I was at home, but as soon as I was out with my friends in public, I felt sick, like I was too shy to eat in front of them. I used to feel self-conscious when eating because I was scared people were judging me, but the truth was no one else cared how much I ate because it did not impact them whatsoever. And maybe other girls may notice and judge, but the reality behind that is girls judge because they themselves are self-conscious. I used to see people eat and say mean comments in my head— I was really targeting myself for wanting to eat more and feeling guilty. One way that I persevered through this obstacle was quite odd, but it worked for me. I filmed myself eating and watched it to become comfortable with eating in front of others. Then as stupid as it sounds, I would compliment myself. It felt kind of good to distance myself from the person on the screen.

In order to push through challenges like this it is important to embrace who you are. You should be proud of who you are including the way you eat, talk, or dance. Ignoring the issues that are placed in front of you is never going to solve anything.

Feeling worthy of love is very important in life in order to feel loved. This was really hard for me because most of my mental capacity was focused on losing weight. My battle was feeling confident regardless of my weight. Fears can consume you and one of the greatest steps you can take is stepping into your fears. Your fears will control you until you are no longer scared.

Part 5: Girl Power

Girl power is about feeling independent, empowered, strong, and confident. I used to feel that way, then I stopped.

In truth, at every turn, the messages coming at me were quite the opposite - that I had NO power and I wasn't enough in the world.

I started believing the messages on billboards, magazines, and social media that I wasn't good enough. I started comparing myself to others to understand myself.

No one else could actually help me feel that I had girl power. I had to look inward to rediscover myself.

This was my journey to rediscovering my own girl power...

Others' Opinions Matter

It was an early spring day, and the air was crisp. I put on my field hockey uniform, like every other girl on my team, and went to play my game. My skirt revealed lots of my legs, not because I wanted to be sexy while playing, but because I hadn't bought a new one and this one was too small. If I wanted to look sexy while playing, I wouldn't end each match with a beet red face and out of breath. I hadn't started to shave my upper legs; it was something that I was nervous about because it was a big decision for me. My mom made sure I knew the commitment it took to upkeep shaving above the knee. During half-time, I noticed a girl staring at my legs, so I quickly crossed them. Then she remarked that she needed to shave her legs to the other girls sitting beside her, and they were all talking about it. I wanted to crawl into a hole and never come out.

The truth was that I listened too much to what others thought - their opinions meant the world to me. Instead of thinking that she probably said that only because she was insecure, I believed that she was sending me a message that I should shave my legs. I wouldn't have believed that unless I already felt insecure about it. The influence that my community had on my behaviour was too big for my own good.

Do you ever put other girls down around you in hopes of feeling better about yourself? Do you ever criticize others' appearances, but you criticize the things you feel most self-conscious about?

I have done those things before; I didn't mean to judge other girls, but my intention was to make myself feel better in a moment of weakness and insecurity, even if it meant putting others down. I remarked on their imperfections in my head and sometimes I didn't even know that I was doing it. I never said them out loud and the truth was I never believed them or even judged them. But when I was hurting, I was more likely to be harsher on the world around me.

If the world continues to sell magazines with models who have large breasts, small legs, and a tiny waist, and women continue to buy them, it creates a beauty standard for one specific body type. Some magazines are really toxic. They might have some good information, but most of it is junk. And the worst part of it is that they are everywhere. The models are often photoshopped and made to look unrealistic, but I kept listening to the messages the media created for me so I would end up wanting to buy products to change myself. This not only causes women and girls to have lower self-esteem but also creates billion-dollar industries out of wasted money on wasted products.

A lot of the time, this pressure to be better came from a voice inside of me that I felt I could not control and would send the message to my head, which made me believe it was true, that I was not good enough and I needed to be better.

In order for me to love myself and love other people, I have to understand myself at my core and be empathetic towards others.

Distinguishing
Reality

Models Are So Much Prettier Than Me

Society and large powerful companies have a major influence on what we, as humans, think. These subconscious beliefs are planted in our brains from a very young age. When the trusted people in our lives tell us something, we believe them. When we were growing up, we were either told things or inferred things based on our experiences and exposure to social media.

I knew the truth about many things, but the truth was I didn't believe the truth. By this I mean, I knew that models on social media edited their photos, but I didn't want to believe they did, and my brain struggled to process it. As a result, I thought I wasn't good enough because I was comparing myself to an unrealistic image.

It all started when I was a kid, and I was told to believe that sunshine and lollipops are happy things. Things that make children smile and elders giggle. The message was reinforced that they are happy things and so that is what they became. But when I was told that they were happy things, it was a single statement that focused on one thing, and it failed to look at the negatives. Sunshine eventually causes sunburns and turns to rain. Lollipops eventually dissolve and can contribute to obesity. So I learned I must value the happy things in the moment because perspectives can change.

Believing that models are ideals, and that sunshine and lollipops are happy things, is only one perspective; it is society's. Giving into someone else's evaluation of things has the ability to create self-deprecating thoughts, as I had when I looked at models. I have been able to acquire the gift of thinking for myself by pausing before agreeing when my brain tells me something. I enjoy thinking critically about things because at the end of the day, my brain is unique to me. I need to protect my own thoughts and limit the influence of external factors as much as possible in order to become who I want to be.

You may find that by paying attention to the world around you, you are influenced by society as well. This is pretty much inevitable because you and I are naturally influenced in order to fit in and understand the culture we live in. But what if we were to pause instead of absorbing what we were told and think about what significant things we have in our lives? What if we were to pause and realize that we actually do not agree with what society, or schools, are telling us to believe?

Inside of us, there is someone with a strong mind and voice that wants to be heard. What if we were to think about the ways that society influences us that we were not aware of before? Maybe it is through magazines, TV commercials, and shows, adverts on YouTube, or Instagram feeds? Maybe most of these things follow us in the little device we hold in our hands every day.

These silent influencers are integrated so deeply into our lives, that we barely notice them anymore, but that doesn't mean they are not there. I found it super helpful to pay attention to my Instagram feed and the impact it had on my life. It may have been hard at first, but learning to distinguish reality was crucial to developing the ability to think for myself.

Judging
Before
Understanding

She Is Trying Too Hard,
Which I Would Never Do

I thought all girls who wore fake nails were popular, stuck-up, annoying teenage girls; I thought the same about false lashes. Of course, this was my judgement of them and it was not even remotely close to correct, but it is the perspective I had of the world at the time.

I never understood why girls got fake nails because they looked uncomfortable and they were expensive. As a result of this curiosity, I decided to get fake nails, just to test the waters. They took some getting used to, and they were kind of impractical, nonetheless, I felt confident when I had them. But the biggest takeaway for me was that I then understood and had knowledge I didn't have before. I understood that fake nails weren't only a piece of luxury, a reflection of wealth, or cute. But they made the girl who wore them feel beautiful and worthy. They made her feel fierce like she could conquer the world with just a piece of painted plastic glued to her real nail. It wasn't about the nails at all, but rather the feelings they evoked inside the girls when they wore them. At the end of the day, it is all about the feelings people get from experiences that keep them coming back or turning away.

Having this knowledge was a shock for me. It allowed me to extend my empathy towards girls who chose this as a preference. I never realized that fake nails were actually a mind game more than anything else. I was able to learn that in order to prevent in-the-moment judgment I had to first obtain information and allow for empathy.

I Can't Accept Compliments

"You're beautiful," someone told her,
But she laughed in response.

The girl accepted the compliment,
Like someone accepts a punch to the face.
The girl stood like a deflated balloon,
She needed air to inflate her balloon,
But wouldn't accept the pump.

The woman who had once complimented this girl stopped,
Like a butterfly with a broken wing stops trying to fly.

The park in which they stood enclosed the woman and the girl,
The trees hung over them as a sense of protection,
Yet the girl's weight shifted from one foot to the other,
As though she was unable to distribute herself evenly.
There were few flowers in this park, the rarity made them beautiful.

The girl scanned the woman in front of her:
She stood like a peacock with outspread wings,
She had amber eyes that echoed the warmth of fire,
Her luscious golden hair danced in the wind,
Like leaves on a tree on a cool fall day.
The woman stood in front of the girl,
Like a lion next to a cub.

She saw the woman's perfect body,

But what made it perfect was that it wasn't hers.

The girl took a step back and looked at the woman.
Then shyly remarked, "well, you're very pretty."
Without a moment of thought, the woman replied, "thank you."
Then the woman walked away like a giraffe sauntering away.

The girl saw the woman as a red rose in a field of yellow tulips.
The girl suddenly felt as though she could walk the beach in her two-piece swimsuit.
She felt the trumpets of her soul resonate throughout her body.

Then she remembered being called ugly.
It made her feel like a weed in a beautiful garden.
It made her feel like a single fish in an ocean full of sharks.

Being called beautiful made her feel like the brightest star on a dark night,
It made her feel like a diamond found within volcanic rock.

The next time a woman said she was "beautiful,"
The girl would smile and say, "thank you."

I'm So Undeserving of Everything

Complimenting another girl can be much harder than it appears. As bad as this may sound, sometimes in the moment that I offered complimentary words to another, I felt emotions of jealousy. Those feelings of jealousy were because they had something that I so desperately wanted for myself.

Once I learned to accept compliments I found that they actually felt amazing and made my day so much better. Even if I didn't completely believe what was said, it still made me feel happier having heard it. I assumed other girls felt this way, too. It obviously depends on the compliment but receiving a compliment can feel amazing because it feels so nice to know that others see your gifts even when you don't see them yourself. I never judge the stranger who compliments me because I see and appreciate the courage they had to speak to me in the first place.

I want to inspire the girls around me, not bring them down. Complimenting other girls is the perfect step to this. I found giving compliments and spreading love could feel just as good or better than receiving because it reinforced my belief that I am a good person in the world because I want to make someone else feel better.

And sometimes I think talking to that person is not a risk I am willing to take because of the fear that they might judge me. Sometimes I find that I haven't even given the compliment and I have gone through seven different scenarios of how it could turn out.

Some of these examples are extremes; however, each one is a realistic representation of my thoughts at the time, and it is important to keep in mind that my thoughts were influenced by the movies I watched. I have also been told many times that I was a major drama queen growing up.

Seven possible scenarios that I imagined for how someone might respond to my compliment:

1) Me: "Wow, you're so pretty"
   Her: "Thank you!"
2) Me: "Wow, you're so pretty"
   Her: "Are you being sarcastic?! Ugh, I'm disgusted by people like you."
3) Me: "Wow, you're so pretty"
   Her: "So physical appearances are the only thing that matter?!"
4) Me: "Wow, you're so pretty"
   Her: "OMG, thank you! I was just thinking about how gorgeous your hair is."
5) Me: "Wow, you're so pretty"
   Her: "Thanks, I model for different brands of makeup so ugly people, like you, can buy it"
6) Me: "Wow, you're so pretty"
   Her: *ignores me*
   Me: *cries inside*
7) Me: "Wow, you're so pretty"
   Her: "I KNOW! Everyone tells me that."

Anyway, every single time I took the risk to compliment someone it went like either scenario one or four. So maybe, just maybe, it is worth the risk after all.

You have probably experienced something I like to call the compliment dance. It is when you see someone gorgeous and then you question whether to say anything. You may let fear overwhelm you and find it hard to make a decision from there. You go back and forth, rocking side to side debating whether to say it or not. Truthfully, if you enjoy receiving compliments then others probably do as well. It is an easy risk to take.

You do not have to worry about what others might think about you because if it is a stranger then you will never see them again. Your courage and kindness have the potential to brighten up someone else's day. It all depends on how you choose to show up in the world at a specific moment in time.

Would you be strong enough to compliment the girl next to you in the elevator? Sometimes, I am not. But when I am, it's totally worth it if it makes someone happier.

Choose
Your
Filter

If She Hates Me Then I Hate Me

On another note, it's a fairly common belief that the female community sometimes does put each other down, and for this situation, there is only one thing we can do. We have to accept it, not take it personally, and acknowledge from whom it came.

When I visited my family friend who exclaimed, "if only there was a beautiful face to go with that hair!" I felt like I had been kicked in the stomach, then punched in the mouth, then covered in car oil, and then just to top it off she dropped a lighter to set me on fire. In other words, this hurt A LOT. I was already self-conscious about my physical appearance; this was not something that I needed to hear.

Even though it killed me to think back on that conversation with her, I knew I had to. I thought about the circumstances: first of all, she was pretty old and a lot of the things she said didn't make sense anyway. She had a habit of saying rude things to people because she thought she was being funny. There was nothing I could do except to know who she was as a person and think to myself, do I respect this person's opinion? The answer was no, so her opinion was no longer valid to me, as she wasn't a trusted source. Trusting an unreliable source to me feels like trusting someone who has repeatedly lied to me. Why would I? I had no reason to believe them.

Two important questions I used to ask myself when I heard another person's opinion:

1. *Is this person a reliable source?*
2. *Do I want to accept this to be true?*

Another thing I learned from this interaction was that no one could put me down but me, and if others did manage to make me feel worse about myself it was because I let them. I don't know about you, but I like winning, and there was no chance that I was going to let someone else win power over me by saying some mean words that I chose to accept as being true.

You might possibly believe an unreliable source. You might also accept the tainted information to be true. And the craziest part is you might not even be aware you are doing it, but you do have the power to put an end to it. You have the power to control your beliefs and validate your thoughts before accepting them as true. You just need to pause. Pausing has great potential to help you realize the world you live in and the things you want to change in your life. Pausing is not about standing still and accepting all of the negative things in the world before moving forward. Instead, it is about learning to create a filter that allows you to acknowledge whose opinion you care about because you should not listen to everyone's opinion. Accepting that you are going to hear negative things is equally important because it is your job to create a filter for your life. What glasses are you going to choose to wear? The yellow ones that emphasize positivity or the red ones that surround you with negativity? It is up to you to choose your filter, every morning of every day.

Part 6: Social Media

Before I was introduced to Social Media, I was confident and clear about who I was in the world. Yet, somehow, I felt that I was missing something important when all of my friends started using it. I felt left out of a bigger world that I desperately wanted to be part of.

I could not possibly have imagined the power these social media apps would hold over me.

I had no idea they would derail my feelings of self-worth...

Social Media Is Everything

Create log in ... done.
Are you older than twelve? Yes.
Click, I'm in!
But I wasn't ready,
But how was I supposed to know?
Welcome to Instagram, they said.

I didn't know girls my age looked twenty-five on screen.
I didn't know I had to post a flawless picture of myself
Every two months, but it could be more often.
I didn't know about the beauty standards
That I felt I had to live up to.
I just didn't know.
I couldn't have known.
Welcome to Instagram, they said.

I began my journey,
I clicked through the accounts and followed friends,
I scrolled the feed until my eyes were square.

I saw couples travelling the world and thought, that should
be me.
I saw photoshopped bikini pictures and thought, that
should be me.
I was twelve and already felt like I wasn't enough.

I was entranced watching others do things,
By the time I surfaced from my phone I felt worse.
But welcome to Instagram, they said.

Days, months, weeks, years passed before I knew.

I knew that even though I knew they were photoshopped pictures,

I didn't believe it.

I knew I didn't feel like enough of anything, pretty or accomplished or travelled,

Because of the stream of social media.

It's
All
Fake

How Am I Supposed to Look Like Her?

I see her perfect face. The face that society believes is stunning. The face that boys like. The face that doesn't look anything like mine.

False lashes, hair extensions, and Photoshop... I did not use them. How was I supposed to compete with girls who did? And how was I supposed to know other girls even used Photoshop? It was so hard to tell and these beauty enhancers were so ingrained in society that they were considered natural beauty, right?

The acrylic nails were fake. The eyelash extensions were false. The beautiful hair extensions weren't real. It was propaganda. I knew it, but I didn't want to process that. These were still the expectations and standards I held myself to. I was ultimately comparing the incomparable.

These unattainable ideals acted as if the world was a masquerade ball. Masks hide you underneath and leave the real you a mystery. Maybe it was better that way, maybe the masks influencers wear were helpful. The truth was that I didn't like them, but I believed them. They fed my inner turmoil and self-deprecating thoughts. The screen behaved as a huge, abandoned field for weeds to grow rapidly and carelessly. Each weed was another unrealistic comparison between myself and others. Unfortunately, the field had unlimited surfaces for weeds to grow. When the surface of the field ran out, the weeds began to pile on top of each other because they always found space.

I knew girls used beauty enhancers, but they were still portrayed as real beauties, correct? It was hard to process the falsity of beauty in a photo. And you believe that, too, yes?

The girls I saw had perfect figures and it made me want to have a perfect figure. Actually, it made me want to have *their* perfect figure. And then there were the girls who were curvy, thin, and tanned, and then I wanted to be them. I wanted any semblance of approval.

I was a child who wanted to be the best of everything I saw. A compilation of the best of everyone. The girls with pretty eyes? I wanted those. The girls with unique dimples? I wanted them. The girls with light, tanned freckles? I wanted them. And what I did have, I wanted it to be better. I had blue eyes that weren't blue enough. I wanted cheekbones, but when I developed them they didn't look the same on me as they look on others so I didn't like them.

Cheekbones, freckles, and curves are all considered natural beauty. These things alone, without the help of makeup and photos, seemed almost invalid and not enough for watchers and scrollers like me.

I sat in my room and thought of the girl in the pink, floral two-piece bikini standing on a beach somewhere in Hawaii that I saw earlier on my phone. She had beautiful long brown hair, bright green eyes, tanned skin, a flat stomach, thin legs, and the list goes on. And then I continued to click. I saw her in France standing in front of the Eiffel Tower wearing a perfectly styled outfit. Then in Australia on another beach, closer to the camera but with no imperfections. I imagined being on a beach looking like her, and I wished that was my reality. The scariest part was I didn't follow her because I liked her, I followed her because I wanted to be her.

Then there were the long hours of scrolling through food, modelling, and travel accounts that were perfectly curated to make me feel dissatisfied with my life. The more I watched others live their lives, the less I lived mine.

Without technology, I might not have had these extreme feelings of not being good enough. I turned off my phone and threw it against my bed as hard as I could without damaging it. I closed my eyes with despair and sulked. I was good at sulking. Honestly, it was my talent. I was the best at picking apart my body piece by piece, to say something negative. If I did that to anyone else it would have been bullying, but I managed to do it to myself quite easily.

I grabbed my phone and opened it back to the social media post. Then I did the unthinkable, I unfollowed the girl who made me feel terrible. The girl who represented everything I wanted to be but could never be without serious plastic surgery. The girl that travelled and made me uninspired. In that moment, I broke the glass surface of my addiction. It was only just the beginning. Then I did something else even crazier: I followed accounts that inspired me to become who I wanted to be. They helped me see the possibilities of places I can travel to and the life I can create for myself through choosing a job I actually enjoy. The materialistic things and unrealistic visuals presented in front of me were no longer constants.

In other words, follow what inspires you. As long as the content lifts you up to become your best self then you are moving in the right direction.

It is so easy to get dragged into the virtual world as an escape, but it is not the most rewarding when you have to turn the screen off. Managing how I spend time on social media every day is really important to me so that my influences are real people in real time, not influencers with a curated life.

I didn't focus on myself and that's what made me love myself more. I didn't have anything to compare myself to if I didn't look at anyone else as competition. I didn't have to hide behind the masks that Photoshop and makeup created. I didn't need to have the picture perfect figure that I saw online. And I didn't need to be curvy with dimples.

Full of Lies
and
False Advertising

The Media Is Real

I knew that social media was full of lies and false advertising, but I still believed social media reflected reality. I always figured that I wanted to believe the lies since, in a way, it gave me a sense of hope for the future. It allowed me to see people being followed and who were liked so I could change myself to be them.

Scrolling social media was like turning on Netflix because, once it was on, it was hard to turn off. It was a dark hole that sucked hours of my time if I was not careful. The stories that are seen when scrolling - the cliffhangers at the end of an episode of your favourite shows, or the feed on Instagram that had skits, or the TikTok's that are always entertaining - kept people, like me, coming back for more.

I created a belief, through stories or ideas, of something that I would then live by as if I had thought this for my whole life. I made up stories in order to keep myself satisfied with my inability to stay motivated. For example, one of my habits was to watch Netflix when I was bored. Another habit was that I would overeat when I was stressed. Of course, consciously I knew that I should not overeat. Nevertheless, the truth was that I had created a pattern within myself to think that when I was stressed, I lost discipline and believed that it was okay to neglect my typical routines and beliefs. When I was stressed or nervous, I made up stories to make me feel better and justify my lack of motivation.

Growing up, between ages one and twelve, my family had a TV, but it was rarely turned on. The TV was in the basement and was on for only three reasons:

1) We were playing Wii (or a game) as a family
2) We were having a family movie night and watching a DVD
3) There was a hockey game on

My parents didn't believe that spending time watching TV was good for you. Instead of sitting in front of the TV after school, I went outside and played with my neighbours in the fort in my backyard. In other words, my parents didn't use television as a babysitter and I'm so thankful. It gave me the opportunity to be creative, to try new things, and to use my imagination with my Playmobil.

Today, people talk about certain TV shows as though they follow them religiously and I never understand. I remember when I got older my mom would come downstairs after I had been watching TV for two hours and ask me to turn it off. I wanted to yell like the world was ending – to be fair, the virtual world I was entrenched in was ending. I was addicted to something even when I barely spent time on it.

Every time I told people I didn't really watch TV (because, in a sense, we didn't really have one) they usually had one response: "That sucks! I'm so sorry for you, you skipped childhood! You missed out!". I always wondered why they would say that, and I realized that it felt to them like I hadn't had a childhood because it wasn't like theirs. Because they had grown up with a TV, they couldn't comprehend a childhood without one. The truth was I didn't feel like I missed out.

When I was able to watch TV, as I grew older, I watched a show called *Victorious*. It was probably one of the most brain dead shows I could have watched - it was targeted at people half my age. I chose to watch it and I noticed Ariana Grande was getting a lot of attention. For some reason, the uniqueness of her voice really stuck out to me. I didn't feel good enough about who I was, and I thought I needed to change and morph myself into the features of other people in order to be liked. So, as a result, I sometimes spoke in a pitch that was ten times higher than normal and it was probably very annoying. I remember my brother pointing it out and I rejected every piece of evidence and told him he was wrong and that I was being myself. I didn't want to tell him that I didn't like myself and I thought that acting like someone else would make me more likeable to myself and others. Looking back, her voice was very annoying in the show, but for some reason, I felt that's what I needed to be. I used other people as stabilizers for myself when I felt like people didn't like me for me.

Social media has had a huge impact on the things that influence people's lives. The influence can either be negative or positive, but either way, it changes how we think, and it changes our perceptions of ourselves and the world. A lot of the time the influence happens subconsciously - I didn't even know that my mind was being shaped to think a certain way by marketers and big companies. I began to feel like my opinions and vision were clouded by new thoughts that I didn't necessarily agree with. Were my thoughts really my thoughts? Was I being influenced to think certain things due to a high volume of exposure to the same things via Instagram? I felt like I was portraying the anger of the news and the attitude of social media influencers, and I really didn't like it. It was scary to think about who I had become without even trying because I wasn't even aware that I was being influenced.

This led me to believe that all social media influencers were really bad because I couldn't deal with the constant sight of them and what they were doing to my happiness. There was an imbalance of good and bad because, for every one good influencer, I would see five negative influencers. They might not have seemed negative at that moment, but it didn't make me happy thinking about their life compared to mine.

Social media decreased my confidence and mental well-being. It was a place where I continued to look at how pretty other people were and see all the things they had that I didn't. The worst feeling I experienced after scrolling on Instagram was when I snapped back to reality and looked in the mirror and had a stronger aversion to myself than when I had started.

You may know that social media is not trustworthy because the photos posted are often heavily edited and photoshopped. And it is a place where everyone posts pictures that tend to reflect themselves at their best. Of course, most people don't post things that show their insecurities. Who would? I didn't want people to see me the way I saw myself, which was an insecure mess. Before posting, I used to ask at least twelve people for their advice, but I was also aware that people don't always feel comfortable sharing the truth, so I never felt that I could fully trust them to be honest. I had to accept that no matter what I chose to post, people were eventually going to see the real me as soon as we met in person.

Trusting what you see on social media is a horrible mistake to make, even if it's an unconscious belief. It is like watching a romantic comedy and believing that this exact situation, step-by-step, could one day, possibly, maybe happen to you. The likelihood of that happening is low and these unrealistic expectations of what life should be like set me up for disappointment in my life.

Social media is a huge advertising platform, which means the purpose behind most posts is to make people feel somehow unsatisfied so they are driven to buy the products being sold. Influencers gain followers to gain sponsorships to sell products, but if I felt perfect the way I was, why would I buy a beauty-enhancing hair gel to hold down my fly-aways? The posts everywhere were designed to make people like me believe that the products they sold would solve my problems even though I knew, on a rational level, that they wouldn't. Maybe buying the lip gloss that IT girl posted on Instagram would bring me closer to achieving what she has? The reality, however, was that it wouldn't. How could it? I wouldn't have her house, her physical appearance, or her money, just by having a product she was being paid to promote online.

All that being said, social media isn't all bad. It's a platform where we can network and connect with others, and it also represents opportunity. It reveals a world that some couldn't even imagine and exposes us to new possibilities of how our lives could be. We can learn from it if we use it that way.

What's most important is that you choose who you follow and think for yourself, otherwise it is easy to be subconsciously brainwashed. Messaging and videos can alter the things that we believe to be true. I can't emphasize enough the importance of questioning what you see and thinking independently. Follow brands, people, and content that encourage you to be your true self.

I'm
Good
Enough

I'm Not Good Enough

It sometimes felt like the thoughts inside my head were telling me I should be what I see on social media even though my rational brain knew it was not realistic. I knew my pressure points and my deepest insecurities which allowed me to self-bully and evoke extreme amounts of emotional pain through the comparison of myself to another. My voice was being fueled by my social media usage. It was harder not to pay attention to myself too because I couldn't exactly walk away; my inner voice nagged like a ghost haunting me.

If someone asked me to list all my insecurities, I could do so endlessly. In fact, thanks to social media, if I ran out of ideas, a few minutes, or hours, of scrolling would introduce me to a whole bunch that I hadn't even considered.

My biggest critic, my inner voice, was emboldened by my Instagram feed and had no problem telling me that I was not good enough. This happened all the time and I listened without question and I began to believe it was true. I allowed myself to get bullied by my most trusted source: me. This happened a lot and not only when it came to bullying myself but also when being bullied by others. For me, it was usually who I trusted most that hurt me the most because I had developed a relationship with them, and I believed what they said to be reliable and valid. This meant that I took to heart what they said more than what I heard from others. It was harder not to listen to people I loved and trusted, especially when I had known them for so long.

The biggest truth I can offer you is that you know you better than anyone else knows you. You don't have to listen to critics, including your inner voice, because they are not always right. You have the ability to not pay attention and quiet the voice that tells you you're not good enough. I know this because I was able to. I found that talking back to that little inner voice was quite helpful in quieting its efforts that I believed were to make me feel worse. As I have grown older I realized that the voice was essentially trying to protect me from being a social pariah. It was using my past experiences to help guide my behaviour in the future so that I didn't make the same mistakes. The voice had some reason for saying what it said, but that didn't mean that it was always right.

I Wish I Was Older

Sitting in my room at fourteen years old, I would wish that I was sixteen years old and free. I thought I would have so much independence at sixteen. By the time I reached sixteen, I wished I was twenty and at university. I imagined at this age, I'd be free to do whatever and wouldn't be living at home anymore. My expectations of what specific ages would bring were never met. I could never have anticipated the new problems that would come to light with each new age.

When was this wishing away my life ever going to stop? When would I realize that being in the present was the best medication for being where and who I wanted to be in the future?

I wished for things because I saw the potential for a better life on social media. Of course, I probably saw only one percent of reality through social media, but I liked to believe the lies I was told because it gave me hope that things would get better in the future. I believed in true love because it was better than not believing at all. It gave me something to look forward to and something I craved in the future. It was not that I wanted the exact life of another person, but I wanted to experience the things they did.

What did I really want in the future that made me want to wish my life away? In reality, I didn't believe I actually wanted my life to be gone so quickly even when it felt like it. In my future's mind, my bubble of perfection had not popped yet, so there was still hope for what I might experience. I thought traveling to another country would make me happy because I saw a post of a woman smiling while travelling in Australia.

It all came down to the conflict between my desire for freedom and my imagination of the perfect future I wanted, and believing that realistically it might not happen like I thought it would. If I wanted to live a life of freedom it started with being proactive in the present. It was the actions I took in the present that created who I became. Sure, I wanted to be dating the man of my dreams, but I didn't really want to do that right now. I was not ready! I could barely even speak to boys my own age without getting super nervous and I wanted the freedom of not being tied down.

If I always hoped to be in the future, I would never reach who I wanted to be because I would have made no progress towards it while I was in the past. Instead of wishing away my life, it was better to take what I learned from the worst parts of my life and use these lessons in the present to guide my strategy for taking on the future. This is where the inner voice in my head that constantly had something to say was helpful because I would be less inclined to repeat history.

Part 7: Stress & Anxiety

How could I have known, as I entered my teenage years, that my lighthearted, carefree days were rapidly nearing an end?

There were signs. I'm sure there were signs.

Except I didn't see them...

Breathe

Feeling the Pressure

Shingles was stressful.
Puking, fainting, crying, yelling,
Breathe, I said.
But my heart raced a little faster,
And my nerves yelped with strain.

Thinking about my future was stressful.
My future was a path on a mountain with millions of
different trails.
But oh, God, what was I doing with my life?
Breathe, I said.
I could do whatever, I could become a
Pilot, painter, lawyer, novelist, doctor, DJ.
I could pick whatever I wanted.

My jittery leg, my heart rate high, my eyes glancing around,
My hands dancing, my head pounding.
It felt like there was nothing I could do,
Like a young elephant being held down by lions as prey.
Breathe, I would say.
Then a quick inhale and back to hyperventilating.
Don't think about it, it made it worse.
Breathe, I said.

Everything was stressful.
It didn't matter what it was, I was stressed about it.
It was as though I was stressed about a burning house,
But I was the one holding the lighter.
Breathe, I said.

I found relaxation in myself, and I took deep breaths without being told,
Like a young elephant accepting its fate and learning to let go.
I scheduled my tasks and worked harder than ever,
As a lion studies its prey.
Air flowed inside of me; I was able to find strength in each breath.

New
Perspectives

How Do I Learn To Let Go

I let stress control my life.

I worried about everything.

And I think in full honesty, I found the stress to be addicting and exciting. I didn't like it, but something within me craved it. I needed to be busy and stress powered my internal drive to work harder. It helped me get things done. Without it, I was not sure if I could be productive and meet deadlines.

So by the time I started high school, my addiction to stress had already started to take hold and I was a disaster in those first couple of years. I had crutches twice which made me decently immobile, my grades weren't great, and I disapproved of my body. My worries ranged from grades, to friendships, to universities, to boys, and to body image - all the things that I felt mattered and defined my future. It was hard to balance everything, especially when every goal of mine seemed impossible to achieve.

In March 2015, during my eighth grade year, I contracted shingles. No, it is not a thing only old people get, but it is rare for a young girl just the same. When stress overpowered me, I tended to break down in every aspect of my life. This was a point in my life where my body was barely functioning. Every bone, muscle, organ, and ligament inside of me had collapsed. One afternoon the itching from shingles became unbearable and I decided to take an oatmeal bath to try to get some relief from it. I knew that if I scratched it could cause scarring, and because of my experience with the scar on my chin, I was petrified of developing more scars. So I got into a hot bath and started to relax. After what seemed like only a few minutes, I began to overheat and something in my body felt wrong. I called out to my mom to come and help because I felt dizzy and she helped me get to my room. I remember saying that I didn't feel well, so she went to the washroom to get the garbage can in case I got sick. She left the room and my energy immediately changed to an inability to function. I felt myself lean forward to throw up, and unfortunately, the rest of my body collapsed with it as I fainted. I blacked out. The next thing I heard was my mom screaming for help while she held me with my face covered in my own vomit. I had collapsed in every possible way.

For years to follow, no one would know this much about me because I wouldn't tell anyone the details. Strangers didn't really know who I was, unless, of course, I introduced myself as the girl who had shingles when she was thirteen.

If I could label myself as the thirteen year old girl who got shingles, could I choose to label myself with something else?

Like what if I said:

Hi... I'm insecure about my stomach because it isn't flat, so I wore one-piece swimsuits for a lot of my teenage years

Hi... I have a scar on my chin because it was a birthmark and it could have gotten big, dark, hairy, and possibly turned into cancer, so I got it removed and have had five surgeries on it since I was born, and I had to wear bandages on my face and other kids pointed at me on the playground.

Hi... I went on a school exchange and got depressed when I was there, so I gained nineteen pounds while I was away for only two months.

This just seems like a call for attention, and I think you get the point... My life was nowhere near perfect but not very many people knew. I wasn't treated differently and instead, I suffered silently.

After I had supposedly recovered from shingles after spring break, I jumped back into school. Less than a month later I woke up to severe nerve pain throbbing through my leg. I was rushed to the emergency room and immediately admitted to a bed. I got an MRI and remember lying flat in that cold and dark machine while holding myself completely still. I was trapped in there for over an hour, feeling alone and scared, and wanted to cry. It felt like my life was over. Once they brought me back out, I was wheeled on a stretcher to the quick turn-over room. I was told that I should remain at the hospital for a couple of nights just to monitor everything.

After shingles, I felt re-born.

Shingles was not the only evidence of when my stress got out of hand. I sweated buckets under my armpits, so I couldn't wear normal shirts due to the embarrassment I would feel. This wasn't genetically-driven sweating because when I was young, I never had an issue, and of course, it developed around the age of thirteen.

Because of my inability to control my stress, I missed school, lost friendships, was constantly sleep-deprived, and, piece-by-piece, things began to fall apart. I began to lose sight of all the things that mattered to me, including a successful future.

As the common saying goes, there's sun after rain, and sometimes you'll be lucky enough to see a rainbow. Stress had hurt me in more ways than imaginable, but it had made me and shaped who I was at that point, and I am eternally grateful for that. Experiencing this type of stress brought me a sense of new found gratitude. I appreciated school and friends more than ever because I knew what it felt like to feel like I was losing everything.

The seed of my stress was all due to my inability to control my emotions. I wished that there was a switch to turn off emotions because I was too sensitive, and I was always the one getting hurt. I needed my emotions to help me make sense of the world around me.

It was not about removing stress, but rather not letting it control you. Gaining control of stress opens opportunities that are otherwise unavailable and ultimately helps us have a better life. But it doesn't come easily, and in all honesty, although this perspective has helped me and I have improved a lot, I am still learning to control my stress.

I'm So Mad

My nerves were tense, AND I was on edge, AND I wanted to cry, AND I couldn't think of anything, AND I was spiraling, AND *everything* was getting worse. All I wanted to do was turn on the TV and watch a show or movie of a perfect life that others had and I didn't, but then this spiral would continue and get faster and worse, and, well, to be frank, it just wasn't good. I had to find something to do to relieve the stress. If I was being 100% truthful, even though I would much rather lie to both myself and to you right now, being on my phone and procrastinating didn't help.

I had to find an outlet. I found that exercise was a pretty good stress relieving method. At least for me. Let me clarify, by exercise, I do not mean the gym. The gym terrified me. I was scared of it. It was wayyyy too intimidating. Exercising for me did not stem from a desire to be healthy. I was motivated to exercise simply because I was angry and needed to place my excess adrenalin into something useful. It allowed me to feel a sense of relief. I could put my headphones in and go for a walk or do something to move my body.

Before I started to exercise more regularly, I resorted to sulking when I was angry. I had a bad habit of doing this when I was having trouble processing emotions or felt that I was getting very agitated by something around me. The best possible solution was to escape, recover, and return, and for me, exercise was a great recovery habit because it helped me get out of my head. To be clear, my main motivation for starting to exercise as a recovery method was to make sure I didn't say something I would later regret when I returned.

My Messy Room Is So Annoying

When my room was a mess my mind was cluttered. It was not exactly calming walking into a room with an unmade bed, clothes on the floor, and school supplies, among other things, stacked on the desk. In fact, it added to my stress, because I felt like I couldn't manage anything. My room was like my own little bubble of clarity; when it was clean then I could think and I was inspired, but when it was messy, oh boy, it was not good. It was a cycle: my room was clean, I got tired, my room got messy, then I got upset and annoyed. The more tired I was, the worse my room got and the more dysfunctional I was when it came to controlling my emotions.

The thing is, I didn't plan for a messy room; it just snuck up on me. I came into my room at night and I was really tired. I grabbed my pajamas and got changed, then I had my clothes that I had worn during the day. It would have taken me fifteen seconds to hang my pants and shirt and another eight seconds to take my underwear to the laundry bin in the washroom, which is where I was going anyway. So, I did just what any reasonable person would do; I thought, "nope I'm too tired", threw my clothes on my bench near my wall or on the floor, and said: "I'll do it tomorrow". That was the start of an uphill battle. I knew it, you probably know it, and it was game over.

Taking all that into account, the first thing I did when I got really stressed was clean my room. This gave me a sense of calm and reassurance that I still had control of my life.

When I felt like I had no control over anything in my life, at least I would have a clean room. That would be something that I could control one hundred percent of the time, so there was no need to stress about it, because I always had the power to change it. I found that when my environment was inspiring, I felt more inspired to do things to help myself.

What Am I Going To Do With My Life?

I always found myself asking, "what am I going to do with my life?", a question that felt extremely stressful and got me worked up.

Even thinking about these basic topics - which I often did for more than ten minutes - stressed me out:

a) *What should I eat for breakfast?*
b) *Should I exercise today?*
c) *Should I read this book?*

Since I couldn't do everything, this is where priorities and boundaries were set based on two things: importance and capability. If things were really stressing me out because I knew I should do them but didn't want to, then the answer was simple: do it. Especially if it was a quick task that didn't take up a lot of time.

My strategy to get things done, however, went beyond the mental discipline required to just do it. I created lists, either online or on paper, and ranked them in importance. When I wrote lists, I wrote micro-tasks that would allow me to feel like I was achieving more things. Also, I would make my task easier to complete, so when I had no motivation to exercise whatsoever, I put on my workout clothes, then got on my phone, then realized I really could be working out and then I began and then I got into it, and finally, I was happy I did it. Getting started took up a lot of time, which wasn't great, but it was an improvement. To cut down on this wasted time it was sometimes helpful to set a schedule for myself, like work out at four pm every day, which didn't give me time to waste an hour.

A second strategy I used was finding a time of the day when I was most inspired and productive. My time is early in the morning because I am super energized and ready for the day. By the time mid-afternoon hits, I have no motivation and no discipline, so I tried to wake up early and take advantage of feeling alive, in my zone, and powerful.

I found, and still find, that managing stress is really challenging. When I didn't manage it, it held power over my emotions. The mindset 'just do it' took away from the long process of procrastination and set the stage for increasing productivity. 'Just do it' was a decision that was made in the moment when I wanted results in the future, but knew I had to overcome the current hurdle in front of me.

Part 8: Assumptions

Often, when we don't know something for certain, we tell ourselves stories to fill in the gaps. The details we choose to include in those stories tell us a lot about ourselves and how we see the world around us. If we choose to create positive stories, they lift and encourage and inspire us.

Except what's the fun in that when you can just as easily spiral into the depths of despair and self loathing by making up details that create negative stories?

These are the stories – the destructive stories – I was telling myself ...

I Look Like A Boy

I was eight at the time, and even though I wasn't a teenager when it happened, it had a big impact on my teenage years. I thought about it constantly and used it to put myself down. I got my hair cut short for the sole reason of loving my brother so much that I wanted to be him. I liked it for maybe a total of ten minutes, and when I got home and looked in the mirror, I collapsed, bawling. I looked like a stray dog; my hairs were uneven and it looked messy.

One day soon after that, my mom picked me up from school, we were both in fairly high spirits, and my mom had to run a few errands. We had to stop at the grocery store and go to the post office.

We pulled up to the parking lot of the small mall and walked in together. We made our way to the post office. It was located beside a dance studio where I had once taken a ballet class, but I found no enjoyment in being told to do things, so I quit. A shiver ran down my spine when we entered the office. Something didn't feel right—it felt like hearing Christmas music in the middle of June. I shook off the feeling, looked at my mom, and knew everything was going to be alright. My mother had ways of looking at me that felt like more than just a stare: I felt understood and safe.

The post office was strewn with boxes of all shapes, envelopes of all sizes, and stamps with many different patterns and images. My mother and I walked through the shop until we reached the counter where we then rang the bell on the desk at the back of the store. As we waited for someone to come out and tend to us, we glanced around. I couldn't help but notice the stacks of filled boxes and the garbage bags full of envelopes. Each box was going to be received and opened and it would be from someone that they knew or loved, maybe a necklace or a care package, or food, or maybe something that someone just ordered online. The envelopes were filled with love letters and friendship letters that people who were in love spent time writing OR maybe it was just a Visa bill, or tax return, or bank statement. I like the story of a care package and love letter better.

A man finally came out from the back of the store: he had a great big smile, white pearly teeth, and wore a uniform. He and my mother exchanged a few words about what she needed and then as my mom was paying, like any worker does, he decided to make small talk. Sometimes people talk when they really shouldn't, or they talk about something too personal - there is a fine line. This man spoke the words that would hurt me like he couldn't imagine. He said to my mom, "I have a boy just like yours, and around the same age, too". He grinned innocently like he had been the kindest man on earth, and all I wanted to do was give him a piece of my mind and slap him silly. My mom chuckled a little nervous laugh like, "uh-oh, he should not have said that," and then held my shoulder as if to calm me down as she explained I was in fact a girl.

I don't want to gender stereotype, but I was wearing obvious girly clothes, including bright pink checkered shorts and a pink top with a butterfly on it. Even when I wore feminine clothes, people only saw what they wanted to see, and they didn't spend time looking past their first impression of my boyish haircut.

I would always remember that moment.

They Are Right

I was called a boy, or I was told I was younger than my actual age, or I was called stupid because of my blonde hair. These were some examples of the assumptions people would make just by looking at my physical appearance. Yes, I had short hair, and I was short, and I had blonde hair, but that didn't make me into the things that people assumed I was.

General assumptions of who I was became more common when I entered my teenage years. Things like height, age, and physical appearance all became suddenly very important to who I was. I never thought they were important, and honestly, they're really not because they hold no actual meaning. Yet oftentimes the people around me used these things to make assumptions and judgments. I wouldn't call these people judgmental for making assumptions, but rather closed-minded. I found that people who made these statements had a hard time changing their minds when they came to a conclusion based on another factor.

People can find a way to make fun of you for just about everything. I learned this the hard way because I wouldn't notice something about myself and then someone would point it out, and then suddenly, I was really insecure. It felt like a trend. It didn't matter what it was about me, but everything was wrong, and because I wasn't confident, each joke hurt a little bit. The more people said it and the more the message would be repeated, the more I believed it without really acknowledging it. I considered it subconscious brainwashing because I didn't realize that the jokes and comments were impacting me on another level.

Being Older Is Easier

I assumed that being older would be easier. When I was twelve I wanted to be sixteen. When I was sixteen, I wanted to be twenty or thirty.

I assumed everyone older than me had their life together.

I assumed life got easier because you supposedly got more independent.

I was wrong.

The desire to be older likely stemmed from people constantly mistaking me for someone much younger than I am.

My biggest pet peeve was when people assumed my age. When walking into restaurants, even at the age of sixteen, I would get asked if I wanted a kid's menu. I have always been short for my age, being five foot one and all.

I have come to believe that the assumptions people make are almost impossible to break because they happen within a matter of seconds. I thought but had no scientific evidence to suggest it, that people saw something, then related it to what they have grown up to believe, and then formed a conclusion based on what they already thought.

When I walked into a restaurant people saw someone short which automatically made them think of youth, and then they assumed my age and didn't really look at anything other than my height. I presumed they focused on my height because they had to tilt their head down to look at me, which caused them physical strain or movement they wouldn't normally have to do. Of course, this was just my interpretation of things, but I did believe it made sense by just thinking about how I reacted when I saw a tall person.

When I expressed a dislike for being mistaken for younger, people would always reassure me that I will look young in the future and age slowly. I hope they are right.

I suppose it doesn't matter what age people think I am, it's more about how I present myself anyway. I often looked down on myself for looking young and felt I had more to prove as someone my age. It was important for me to realize others' assumptions of my age were not a reflection of my maturity level.

I learned not to assume others' lives were easier. The older I got, the more I discovered that adults had more obligations, and I began to appreciate being young and free from immense responsibility.

You Are So Sensitive

Without self-acceptance, I found that others' words hurt more than they should, even if they were jokes. If I knew that what they said was inaccurate, and deep down I believed that others' words couldn't hurt me unless I let them, then I felt in control of my life. People might have assumed that I was twelve years old but that shouldn't have hurt me like it did.

I once heard that someone will always be better at something than you and I do think that this is true - you can't control that. There is one thing; however, that I can control, and I believe you can, too. I believe that I am the best at knowing myself when I really consider who I am, and you can be the best at knowing who you are too. Getting to know myself was really tricky, and when meeting new people, I always found it hard to stay true to myself, but I am the best at knowing who I am, what my needs are, and who I want to become... and when failing to listen to my true desires I like myself a little less.

In order to accept and process the rude comments about me, I had to learn to acknowledge them instead of being in denial. And I mean truly think about the rude comments.

Some of the rude comments I heard quite often include:

- *You are so sensitive*
- *You look 12*

- *Don't expect much from a blonde*

By thinking about the comments I was able to come to the realization that what anyone else said wasn't true. I could throw it in the 'mind trash' and not think about it again. But in order to realize that they were wrong, I felt like it was important to listen first.

You might find yourself listening to and putting so much value on others' feedback because it means the world to you. To overcome this, listening is a must, but you do not have to change who you are or accept rude comments as though they are true.

I Wish I Was Perfect

The statement *nobody is perfect* is too accurate, and if that isn't the truth then I don't know what is.

I knew I wasn't perfect. This didn't mean I was not beautiful and it didn't mean I was not smart. I was just not perfect. A perfect person would have read all the books in the library. I had not, and I knew relatively nothing. By accepting that, I was able to realize perfection was impossible. When wearing a two-piece bathing suit, I used to feel really REALLY uncomfortable showing my stomach. Why? Because it was not perfect. But when was anyone else's stomach perfect? I mean, seriously. What even is perfect? The word 'perfect' is used so often, but what does it really mean? Instead of saying 'it's not perfect,' because that is a general statement, why don't we question what would make it perfect? Does perfect mean it is flat, curvy, round, scarless? This questioning of perfection allowed me to learn what my version of perfection was and the underlying reasons for this definition.

Nothing is perfect, and I had accepted that because there was nothing else that I could do. If people were going to make jokes about me, more specifically about my height, then I was going to joke with them. People still make fun of my height, A LOT, and even back then when I didn't like the teasing, I had learned not to care one little bit, so I joined in on the jokes. I did this then, and I still do it now, because it showed other people that I did not feel pain in their words, and I had accepted it as well. Joking back with them usually caught others off-guard when they made fun of me because people didn't usually join in when they were the center of that kind of joke. I wasn't sad about my height in the first place so their words couldn't hurt me, it would be like someone telling me I was wearing the ugliest yellow nail polish, but my nails weren't painted. It wouldn't hurt me because I knew it was not true.

If anything, don't let ego get in the way of life's reality. Acceptance of myself allowed me to joke and play with others, and they learned I was funny and confident. I didn't have to think that I was perfect in order to love and joke about myself. It was not about being perfect that made me enjoyable to be with, but rather my unique personality that attracted people the most. Accepting people's laughter and jokes as a way of connecting with me, rather than bullying or tormenting me, helped me put things in perspective and take life a little less seriously.

I Know What Their Life Is Like

Every day of our lives we make assumptions. Well, at least I do. I'm assuming that I'm not the only one because I've seen others do the same.

I really didn't like it when people assumed things about me, so I tried to never assume things about others. I lived by the saying, 'treat others the way you want to be treated'. I really do believe that being nice to others is great karma for the future.

Realizing that I was making an assumption was one of the first steps in stopping myself from doing it because the majority of the time I was not even aware that I was. One of the worst assumptions I made that I couldn't help making was assuming the accuracy of the life they portrayed on social media. I created a story of their life based on a picture. For example, fake nails and eyelashes—she's obviously a popular mean girl. She drives a nice car, she's a spoiled rich kid. She's going out to eat, and she's going to starve herself tomorrow. She has a good sense of fashion which means she's got money, and she purchases from fast fashion clothing stores like H&M. I've already made four assumptions and I didn't know anything about this girl. I think that, in part, my assumptions came from jealousy, because I wanted to wear fashionable outfits and have a car, too, but some things were just not affordable.

You probably make thousands of assumptions a day without even thinking about it. The scariest part is that most of the time, you don't have control over your initial thoughts. Your thoughts are influenced by your habits, experiences, and exposure to the world.

If you don't know the man walking down the street towards you, you may make assumptions based on your experience of the world. For example, you may think of the man as someone you should fear or you may see a man who looks like your grandfather. You will not see what the person beside you sees because they have not only been exposed to different things but also had experiences at times and places that were different from yours. Your assumptions come to you naturally, as they do everyone else. It is your past experiences that influence the assumptions your mind makes without your noticing. Your assumptions shape how you present yourself in the world, as they reflect your core beliefs, values, and unconscious mind.

Part 9: Relationships

Our relationships are the keys to our happiness. They support us, fulfill us, and nurture our spirit. When you go through your teenage years, every single relationship you have gets redefined. It is a time when friends come and friends go and there is incredible instability at a time when you are desperate to be around people who just understand and accept you.

These are the stories of the instability I faced in my relationships during my teenage years...

I Need To Learn To Let Go

I lost my favourite hat when I was seven,
I can't remember where it was taken, forgotten, or vanished.
I still think about it sometimes, I didn't like losing things,
It made me feel powerless.

I told my friend the truth,
She spat at me in disgust.
Losing her felt numb,
Altering the information that I once held true.
I shut her out, a splash of cold water hit my face in the early morning.
The water droplets sunk into my skin with relief: I'm ready.

I told myself the truth,
But I almost never listened.
I almost never wanted to confront problems but I did,
And it felt as though a weight was lifted off my shoulders.
Like a bird with a broken wing nursed back to health.

I told myself the advice I needed to hear,
I knew what I needed to understand.
It didn't come from a parent or a multi-millionaire motivational speaker.
It came from me.

Friendships
Will
Change

I Don't Want To Lose Friends

I have lost many friendships along the way. It was a challenge to overcome the blame I placed on myself for the loss of those relationships. Without my friends, I would feel disconnected from the world, and sometimes, even with them, I still do.

Friendships are like lemonade. Sometimes when there isn't enough sugar, the taste is bitter. At this point, the friendship is feeling tedious, one-sided, boring, and ultimately unfulfilling. And other times it could be like sweet lemonade as it had too much sugar. At this point, the friendship is thriving, adventurous, amazing, happy, and emotionally fulfilling, but maybe a bit too much. I could almost always tell when my lemonade wasn't real (by 'real' I mean just water, freshly squeezed lemons, and a little bit of sugar mixed together) just like I could with relationships. Friendship is about finding a balance of what you want, just like balancing the ingredients of a perfect lemonade. Interestingly, people enjoy different types of lemonade.

A big thing that greatly supported me in finding friendships I valued and made me a better person was to try to notice my energy after leaving their company. I felt like my brain tricked me into believing whatever it wanted when it wasn't really accurate. Yes, I have been close to people and then figured out that I didn't like spending time with them because they made me feel bad about myself, not on purpose, but spending time with them did not feed my soul. I was nice to them at school and I never ignored them, but I invested less time and effort into these relationships.

Another really important thing I learned in order to manage relationships with more than just my friends was that I couldn't change people as much as I may have wanted to. Friends were in my life to party and laugh with, but I also needed friends who I could chill and cry with. And most of the time these friends were different people depending on what I needed to feel supported. For such a long time I was trying to force girls to be the kinds of friends, and people, that weren't natural for them. Eventually, I realized that I couldn't force people to be the kind of friend they couldn't be because they didn't have it in them to be the way I needed. I experienced this a lot with my brother when he didn't react the way I wanted him to, and it broke me because I felt hurt. When he didn't say 'I love you', I felt hurt, and I knew he was a different person from me, but what I didn't realize was that he expressed it in another way. Instead of saying it, his way of showing me love was coming up to me and tackling me to the floor. I didn't understand that until recently.

When one of my friends was being talked about behind her back, she came to me wondering what was wrong because she felt distanced from everyone. As much as I didn't want to talk to her about our group's friendship problems because there was a risk of us both getting hurt, I knew it was the right thing to do. So, I went for coffee with her and I told her EVERYTHING. I also offered solutions, because simply stating problems wasn't going to help anyone. After that she was able to connect with the girls in my friend group; however, she didn't really speak to me after that. I felt like she was shooting the messenger. We were never close again after that. But maybe this was OK, maybe our friendship wasn't meant to be. Sometimes I would tell a friend the truth and lose them, and sometimes our relationship would get stronger. Friendships were really hard, especially as a teenager, probably partially because parents weren't planning the playdates anymore. And bonding with others wasn't as simple as walking up to someone on the playground and saying "wanna play soccer".

Friendships will change, they will collapse, and they will be built. I have a friend who I have known since kindergarten, and I have a friend who lives in Germany who I spent three months with when she was on exchange at my school and I felt like I had known her my whole life. And I have a friend that started on unfriendly territory when I first met her in grade eight, but now she is one of my strongest friendships.

There is no way of telling when you're going to connect with someone, but when you do, those friendships last if you want them to and if you are willing to make the effort.

I Want To Run Away

During my early days of high school, everyone thought I had the perfect family. I had two married parents, a nice house, and an older brother who would bring home his hot friends.

My friends loved my parents and would always engage with them when they came over, and they would say "I love your parents" and I'd say, "haha... same". I did love my parents and I thought they were pretty amazing, and I have a great relationship with them, but my life was nowhere near perfect. My mom and I were able to spend hours together and never got bored, and our fights diffused fairly quickly. My dad and I are very similar, so we laughed a lot and related easily to each other. But one of the things I also got from my dad is obstinance, meaning that when we would fight it could turn into a world war in our house. There was yelling and then crying and then more yelling, and it wasn't even close to perfect—but why would I tell my friends that? My friends only saw me come home from school and get a snack. They thought my family life was perfect. No family is perfect, not even the ones that look perfect from the outside. What they didn't know was that I wasn't always happy. Sometimes, I was so overwhelmed by all my emotions that I couldn't stand it.

I tried to run away at least six times during high school. I bolted out of the house after throwing on some shoes and slamming the door, usually around dinner time, so it was getting dark. I would sit in the middle of the street or just keep walking away as far as possible until I either turned around on my own or my mom got into the car to come and fetch me and talk through it. It was not the same kind of running away that I did when I was six, where I would start packing a suitcase and my parents would offer to help, which drove me insane. It was the thirteen to seventeen-year-old running away. The age where I was old enough to know directions to where I was going and be safe enough to be outside alone, but too emotionally charged to think rationally and control my behaviour.

I think I was trying to run away from myself and my emotions more than I was running away from the intensity of the situation that was happening at home. But at the time it didn't feel that way. Sometimes my home life just felt like too much.

I felt like those around me judged me and thought I had it easy because they saw the smiley me instead of the one who cried when I got home. I knew I didn't know what others were going through because most people didn't really know what I was going through.

Other people outwardly expressed to me that my parents were perfect yet I felt like they drove me crazy. Experiencing these conflicting opinions of what I knew and what others thought allowed me to develop empathy for others' situations.

Being Vulnerable is Scary

When I wanted to build a relationship with someone, anyone, I tried to remember to be vulnerable. It was pretty easy to say "I want to be vulnerable", but much easier said than done when I felt like everyone was going to judge me for it.

Being open about ourselves creates many opportunities that wouldn't otherwise be there. Being vulnerable is what a lot of people are scared to do with their friends and within communities. Vulnerability is not the same for everyone. Sometimes sharing something vulnerable for ourselves can seem mundane to others, and this goes the other way as well. I may feel like I'm being vulnerable by telling my friend about a fight I had with my brother, yet if they are an open person themselves, they might think of it as just another everyday conversation.

I was in grade nine and spring break had just ended, so in our homeroom groups, we went around and spoke about how we had spent our breaks. Some classmates discussed how they travelled to Europe or Hawaii, and others mentioned how they stayed at their vacation homes. I didn't think about what I was going to say because it just came out. I didn't make up a story and I didn't pretend to be someone I wasn't. I told them exactly what happened. The heater in my house broke right at the beginning of spring break so my family and I spent the whole time freezing, and I wore six layers of clothes and wrapped myself in blankets. I still enjoyed it because my family spent a lot of time together in the kitchen - it was one of the only warm places in the house. My classmates and teacher started laughing at how ridiculous it was and probably at how surprised they were that I mentioned something so minor compared to everyone else's.

But at the end of the day, I didn't share those stories to impress them, but rather to be honest and true to who I was and what I stood for. I'll be honest, I did care what my classmates thought, but I didn't care enough to change who I was.

I was vulnerable in my group because if I wanted to receive honesty in return, I knew I had to release it into the world. One of my closest friends, who I absolutely adore, told me that this was one of the reasons she wanted to be friends with me. She knew I kept it real, and I wasn't trying to be anybody else. Vulnerability is the key to connection.

Vulnerability can build a bridge of connection. It can offer an opportunity for others to relate to us. Vulnerability can be a superpower.

The cool thing is that everyone has the ability and power to use vulnerability. It can especially be a superpower when no one else is willing to try and you can use this to your advantage. So many things that I experienced from being vulnerable did not seem related to a positive result in the future, but I found out later that they were actually very related. After I started my blog, I won an award at school with a cash prize. That spring, COVID-19 hit. I got a job offer and, in the interview, I was told she was inspired by my blog. Vulnerability can open many doors in your future if you are willing to let it.

My Friends Aren't What I Need

I have learned three EXTREMELY important things about friendships:

1. Not all of them last.
2. Never let friends have power over me.
3. There are different friends for different things.

Not every friendship lasts and that's okay, and accepting that was hard for me because I always liked to be friends with everyone. To be honest, sometimes I arrived home after being at someone's house feeling sad and unfulfilled. Neither of those feelings should be felt if I were truly with a friend, so I decided to cut back on time spent with them.

In grade six I had a best friend, but by the time I reached the beginning of grade seven, I began to want to explore other friendships, too. Instead of approaching her, because I had no idea how to tell her "I don't want to be best friends anymore, maybe just friends because I want to meet more people", I used the only approach I knew how. I ignored her, which was probably the worst thing I could have done to a friend. We ended up going for counseling; she still barely talks to me to this day, and it has been six years. Friendships fall apart for different reasons and that is okay. Whether it's growing apart, a fight, moving away, or lifestyle differences, it is normal for people to come in and out of your life. There are billions of people on this earth, and a couple of high school friends would not make or break me.

Holding onto the friendships that weren't working took a toll on me. If I were to still feel awful after my many apologies and attempts to reconcile, then I would not be able to accept myself today. Sometimes we have to let go and accept the loss of a friendship. I had to acknowledge that I had done everything I knew how to do to try to make us better, and that I had to move on without letting her have power over me. I couldn't cry every time I walked past her and said 'hi', and she ignored me. I found that once I had done my part, I needed to let go, otherwise, it would have remained a toxic one-way relationship that I was maintaining for no real purpose. A fire can't burn without wood, so if I continuously threw wood onto a fire, it would expand and grow, maybe even out of control. I found that relationships were like taking care of fires, they required effort and could also get out of control easily; however, they also keep you warm. I couldn't let myself take her actions personally since they then held power over me. I needed to be mentally at peace.

Not all my friends would be there for me when I cried. Not all my friends would be there for me when I had good news I wanted to celebrate. Both; however, are important to have. We need people in our lives who support us through thick and thin. We need friends who cry with us and go out with us, laugh with us, and celebrate with us. My biggest realization was acknowledging that I couldn't force people to be the kind of friends they weren't. I learned to enjoy people's company for who they could be. Those friendships, where a friend was there through everything - the good and the bad, I cherished.

When choosing your friendships, you are in control. You don't have to spend time with people who don't inspire you. You don't need to continue watering a desert. Friendships may change over time, as you grow out of old friendships and into new ones. Sometimes it isn't about the number of friends you have, but rather the quality. I found that one friend who really knew me was more fulfilling than twenty friends who didn't really care about me.

My Goals Are Crazy

The most important relationship you will ever have is the one with yourself.

I discovered a way to develop a relationship with myself. I learned to engage in activities that brought me joy. I learned to try. Trying new things allowed me to uncover my interests and learn more about myself.

Most people are passionate about something, even if it is very small. Sometimes I think the word *passion* is overrated. To me, passion begins as a simple interest or curiosity, which grows as you deepen your knowledge. It starts with trying something new and gradually transforms into a mastery as you continue to learn and engage with the subject. A passion can be just a general interest or a goal you want to achieve.

Sometimes I find that my goals are crazy, too small, or stupid. Yet, I found writing down my goals allowed me to be reminded that I had something to look forward to in the future. This allowed me to create a positive relationship with myself as I was more inclined to do things that would put me in this position.

No matter how big or how small and how broad or specific my goals are, they are in my life because they are a dream or a desire of mine. Dreams reflect who we are at our core.

I always write my goals down even if I choose not to pursue them because I find them later and think, "wow, that's actually something I want to do". I have random lists of goals and bucket lists in many journals, and each time I review them, it reminds me of what I wanted to do at some time in the future.

Here are some examples of goals of mine:

- Study/Work in another country (i.e U.K, Japan)
- Drink eight cups of water a day
- Design my own house
- Exercise 3 times a week
- Get into a top university
- Painting/drawing once a week
- Make other lives better
- Be financially free

These goals allowed me to form a strong relationship with myself and they symbolized the importance of certain things in my life. I know the saying is 'treat others the way you want to be treated', but I couldn't treat others with love and respect if I didn't feel worthy or value those qualities for myself. This led me to believe that coming to terms with myself was the first step to happy relationships with others.

Your goals will be different because your influences have been different up until this point in your life. You may think your goals are crazy, not big enough, or not worthy, but they are your goals. Something that you strive towards achieving or reaching is never stupid. It is the beginning of finding your passion and imagining success for yourself. As you continue to write your goals you may even find that you are discovering more of yourself than you've ever known. Your goals reflect who you are and who you want to be.

I Can't Face My Fears

Another relationship that should be recognized is the one you have with your community. I hear a lot of motivational speakers who say, "don't pay attention to what people say". This information is great and it's a good reminder, but I wonder whether it really helps. Like yes, I agree that you shouldn't worry about what others say, but so many times people who say that don't address how to do it. It's as though someone tells you to start eating healthy, but you do not know what a healthy diet looks like. It could be chips and guacamole or a vegetable stir-fry. You may not know what healthy is until people tell you how to do it. So how am I supposed to not worry about others' opinions? It's not like I can snap my fingers. It is important to learn how and the process needs to be clear instead of just saying a sentence that is supposed to inspire people.

It can be important not to reject all the opinions of others and instead recognize who you trust and who you care about. Listen to the voices of people you respect who share your values and let those be your filter. Good filters help you trust and take your own advice because most of the time you already know what you have to do but your confidence might be clouded because you're scared. Take your own advice and thoughts for the change you want and write down the things you want to tell yourself and then say them back to yourself. I often do this in my head without writing them down. Share your wisdom with yourself.

For example, if something terrifies me, then I'll probably do it. At the end of grade eight, once stress had fully consumed me, I was moved into a separate test room to take assessments. Writing exams or any type of assessment in class stressed me out so much that my brain would freeze, and I would forget everything I had studied. The school chose to move me to the IND room, a test taking room where students went to be alone for complete silence and extra time. It helped when I needed it, but I realized that this couldn't be a long-term thing. I knew that I would have to outgrow my stress about exams - it was taking over and growing into a bigger fear. I knew that when I went to university, I would be writing in a room with far more people and that this was not sustainable. As a result, I had two choices:

1. I could continue to write my tests and exams in the small room and I would potentially become too terrified to ever return to the main test-taking room with the others.

Or

2. As much as it scared me in the moment, I could just jump right in and start writing every single one of my tests in the room with everyone else just to get over myself and to see that it wasn't actually that bad. I was aware that the more that I pushed myself away from the main room, the scarier it became to go back.

I chose option two. Before I felt ready to go back to writing tests in the room, I just went back. I dove right in while the water was still cold. And was it worth it? YES, it was. Would

I do it again? Of course I would! It feels amazing to have tackled a fear that wasn't even that hard in the moment because it hadn't grown into something bigger.

Fears can begin to consume every inch of your body if you do not face them. Your fears are more terrifying in your head than they are in real life. The expectation or memory in your head creates the illusion of something completely awful, when in reality it isn't that bad.

The other day I watched a video of people with phobias who were explaining why they had the phobia. Every single one of them had a past experience that had traumatized them, and instead of facing it again, they blocked it out and pretended nothing had happened. Now they are all terrified of their fear.

Fears will eventually take over if you let them. You can choose to face the harsh reality or cover yourself in a sugar-coated fairytale whilst living in fear. The decisions you make in your life are always up to you.

Stop Being Weird

At the age of fourteen, I got really awkward when talking with people my age. I always felt intimidated and didn't really know what to say. I am embarrassed to say this, but whenever somebody would ask me something I would respond and then laugh uncomfortably. In fact, I was a master at laughing uncomfortably. I had so much experience being uncomfortable with who I was that it just flowed out of me before I could control it. Because I wasn't confident, I felt like I wasn't worthy of saying anything, which led me to giggle nervously because I didn't know what to do. At times like that, when I felt nervous and uncomfortable, my palms would usually get very sweaty, so shaking people's hands became embarrassing and I would try my best to avoid it as much as possible. I remember my brother used to say, of course from a place of love, "stop being weird". And my mom and dad used to say, "just be yourself". I didn't know who I was, and I didn't know how to stop being weird, so I just accepted that I was weird— well, at least I was weird with people my own age.

Relationships are like business transactions but without the exchange of money. When building relationships, people think they need to advertise what they offer. When people first meet, they advertise themselves by saying who they are, but they rarely make an effort to draw on a commonality in this newfound relationship. I tried to be less awkward by taking on the mindset that I didn't care what others thought about me, but that just wasn't true. I did care and I always would. When I had this mindset, I alienated others around me because I gave the impression that I didn't need them. Relationships were so, so, so important for my mental health, whether I liked to admit it or not, and the mindset of caring about others made a difference in how I felt when meeting new people.

To create a connection with someone it is important to speak the language of the person in front of you. People who know they need to do this react differently when they first interact with someone. Instead of showing up and not saying much, they guide the focus of the room. They introduce themselves, say something interesting, and ask the other person about themselves. While listening they engage with the person, by asking questions and being genuine in the conversation.

The truth is people like talking about themselves. In other words, engage the person with themselves, because there is rarely something more interesting to most people than themselves and their own stories. Letting others tell a story and then sharing one of our own offers great insight into who each of you is and helps build a connection between you.

People tell stories all the time. It is ingrained in our lives because our experiences form our understanding of the world. Telling stories is at the center of human connection and deepens interactions with others.

I grew up in a household that has held many of my parents' business events. Meaning I have had loads of practice networking and have learned so much by studying the interaction and body language of people in the room. I knew how to interact with adults, and I felt more comfortable doing it. But other teenagers... pffff. I had no idea what I was doing, and as soon as I interacted with other teens, my maturity level dropped a thousand levels. I usually tried to match the others' energy in the room, which took so much effort and didn't allow me to be who I wanted to be. With adults, like my friend's parents, I could talk with no problem and feel at ease. I guess the pressure from peers my age really drove me to insanity.

I realized I had to stop changing myself in order to match others. I lost some friends by doing this. I still cared for them, but the truth was if they didn't like that I felt confident with who I was then why would I want to be friends with them? A lot of people choose to take the safe road, where they fly under the radar, always staying within the boundaries that others set for them. Being different and unique sets you apart from others, it doesn't necessarily make you weird.

I used to feel like I had a hard time connecting with people in the world around me. It was much easier to accept that I didn't like interaction and stay in and watch Netflix, but trust me, this was not rewarding. Communicating and connecting with others is in our nature. It would be pretty hard to go about in this world without interacting with others, connections are very important to growth and achieving success.

I eventually learned how important it is to be different to stand out. I chose to be myself instead of changing myself to be more like others because it deepened my connections with people in my network and I felt a stronger sense of community with those around me. I had to learn to be my authentic self, weird and all, and use my vulnerability to connect with others.

Your world is limited to your current connections and the ones you are willing to make. It is hard to go through life alone - good relationships are essential to feeling a sense of fulfillment and happiness in life, at least for me. Your network of people exposes you to new opportunities and perspectives and positive connections are essential to helping you create the future you want.

Part 10: Idealizing Life From Movies

OMG! He is sooo cute! And kind. And funny. And loving. And willing to express and talk about his feelings.

Oh, and she is sooo put together! And pretty. And smart. And strong. And successful.

And their lives are so full of fun and adventure and – did you see how they met? So cute, right?

That's what *I* want!

Oh, but life as a teenage girl was sooo very different from what was portrayed in those movies...

Love
Is A
Real Rose

I'm in Love

I sat down on the cozy couch in my living room with one of my best friends. We had some popcorn and an assortment of chocolates and ice cream in order to create a full movie-going experience. And on really good days we walked up to Dairy Queen or made ice cream sundaes at home. We always planned to watch the newest rom-com released that week. We did this almost every Friday, and if there wasn't a new one released then we found another. I was always curious to see how this next movie would take my heart on a journey. Would my heart be breaking and then sewn back together? Would it be carried on a predictable journey?

I didn't know, but what I always knew was the ending. Somehow, they would always end up together. I loved it! It felt like the only thing predictable in my life, at times.

The endings were known before the movies started, yet I continued to watch them. Why? Because I wanted to see the journey and know the path. I wanted to experience the emotions the characters felt. I wanted to experience the feeling of being loved and knowing it wasn't impossible. I knew the idea of perfect love without at least some conflict was impossible. Two people together will inevitably have disagreements. I believe that what makes love stronger are the challenges and getting through the tough patches.

As expected, this next movie had a cute guy and a beautiful girl, and I was looking forward to it. Like all the others, I expected this movie to start with back-and-forth banter or conflict between the two, with an undeniable hint of sexual tension. Or maybe this movie would be one where they are unaware of their love but work on something together and end up falling in love. As a rom-com addict, I knew the writers used tension to create an elongated amount of time where I felt part of the journey and anxious about the outcome (even if I already knew how it would end).

The male lead in the movie looked so suave when he walked. His perfectly textured short brown hair held in place throughout the show. His hazelnut eyes glimmered in the sun and twinkled when he looked at the lead woman. I wanted someone who cared for me the way he did for her. I wanted someone to bring me roses and chocolates and ice cream when I was sad. I wanted someone to know exactly when to kiss me and when to leave me just like he did. I wanted a man who understood me and could read my mind even though I knew the scriptwriter told the guy what to say and how to act. But I still wanted to be treated the way she was by him. I wanted the never-ending money they had to spend on dates, and I wanted the town's fair to be perfectly timed with our dates, where we would happen to wander in and he'd win me a big stuffy and we'd go on roller coasters and he'd hold my hand. I may have been getting a little carried away, but my thoughts always did.

But if I wanted that guy, I needed to be that perfect girl. That girl who had perfect hair, personality, and fashion. The full package never had any flaws. But frankly, I'm not that girl. It would be impossible to be. So, does that mean I'm not worth it? Does that mean love is restricted to just those who are perfect? I thought it was, and I had accepted I would never find love, as one might after watching that kind of movie.

Looking at everyday couples on the streets at home made me realize that none of them were perfect. People have problems and they don't disappear at the end of the movie. The people walking along the streets weren't models and had a budget for fashion that any normal income would provide. Yet these people lived a life together with unconditional love. These random people, in a way, lived a better life. They made their own story, and they loved each other in a way that worked for them. Even if love wasn't having a guy show up at their house with fifty-five red roses and a box of chocolates.

Maybe they expressed love when they rubbed your back or held your hand. Or when they made you breakfast. Or when they gave you a kiss before leaving to remind you that they loved you. Maybe it was simply smiling at each other when waking up in the morning after opening their eyes.

I like to say that in movies, love is like a rose, but more of a cartoon edition: no thorns, perfect petals, never wilted. In reality, love is also like a rose, but a real rose, with thorns and all. It could even be argued that the implications of the pain from the thorns helps keep the rose healthy and reminds us how delicate and precious roses truly are.

I have learned that reality is better than the movies.

I Want a Different Life

I so desperately wanted to be the girl in the movie.

You know, in the movies, where the girl meets a man, and they fall madly in love, and after resolving one small issue, their life is perfect in the end? And I knew how completely stupid it was, but I still hoped that this would happen to me, even though I went to an all-girls school and no guy would ever serenade me from the school bleachers or build me a dream house from scratch (if you know these references, you know what I mean).

By spending every Friday night watching 'chick-flicks' in my pajamas alone or with friends, I had changed my life completely. By watching movies of all the same genre, I had created a false reality in my head that influenced who I was. I had been subconsciously feeding my brain with messages that weren't always aligned with what was important to me.

I gained feelings of hope from watching these movies, which made it almost impossible for me to accept reality. No one would ever be good enough, because I was basically in love with an idea.

I found that I was usually in love with the idea more than the reality. I loved the idea of travelling the world, possibly with a couple of my closest friends, but flying hurt my ears, I could get lost in a foreign country, and I could face any number of unpredictable challenges. And yes, I wanted to go to Italy to find the man of my dreams because I heard the men there were *really* good looking. And oh, my goodness YES, I wanted to live the dream in New York with a group of friends. But the truth was, I didn't really want that. My irrational brain, influenced by my emotions, was telling me that I would give anything for that, but the real question is: would I really want that if I got it? The expectations I set for myself became quite depressing when I really thought about the possibility of them actually happening.

I think that damaged relationships are like that - they are built on an idea and the inability to accept reality. One of the questions that I have wondered about is: Why are there so many divorces? I believe it is due to the fact that people are never satisfied with one another, or people don't want to push through the hard times, or both. I think it's partially due to unmet expectations and the inability to communicate. People may enter a marriage thinking that the relationship is going to be easy. People want the fantasy without living through the emotional strain to get there, and if we're being honest, who wouldn't? It is also easy to idealize a relationship with someone else if you are not with them. This may lead to partners leaving to be with someone else but still end up feeling unsatisfied.

So why was the movie industry pumping out romantic comedies so quickly? What good does it do? The film industry produces these movies like they are going out of style because it feeds the ideal idea for relationships - people like to see the potential for a better life. It is easy for people like you and me to get pulled into the false reality and remain there for a while.

By constantly watching movies that support an ideal idea for you, you may find that you are feeding your brain the wrong kind of information because it supports a lifestyle you don't truly desire. Just like a body can't run on junk food, this is where food for the mind is important. If you wouldn't eat junk food every day for dinner because you knew it was bad for you, then if you knew you were feeding your mind some type of poison, would you continue to do so? Watching movies all the time influenced me through a slow process of constant subliminal messaging and I didn't notice the change in me right away. It took time for me to realize I felt unsatisfied with my own life after comparing myself to these movies. Which means that people like you and me continue to watch them because we may not see an immediate impact.

As much as I wished that I could escape into the movie, it was not going to happen. It turned out these movies were not the good influence I needed at the time.

When I felt myself wishing too hard to escape reality, I learned to take it as a sign to decrease my consumption time of romantic comedies.

I'm Supposed to Do This

Watching these movies damaged my ability to see my life for what it was.

I was almost seventeen and I had never been in a serious relationship before. I felt kind of stupid. I met a boy and decided it was time. I had been brainwashed to believe that the first boy I ever went out with was supposed to be my soulmate. In reality, he was a nice guy but he wasn't really even my type, let alone my soulmate. Instead of taking the time to think about what I felt, my feelings felt foggy and unclear. Being around him made me extremely uncomfortable, nevertheless, I convinced myself it was fine because of all the signs.

The signs:

- He played hockey = It was meant to be
- He had brown curly hair = It was meant to be
- He had a sister = It was meant to be

In hindsight, the signs were not the most logical, yet I created them out of desperation for a relationship.

I didn't dig deep into how I really felt and instead placed every single one of my decisions on a sign. Really stupid thing to do, if I do say so myself.

We had mutual friends, so I thought that meant something. I'd known him for a long time. I thought maybe this was a sign. As soon as the word "maybe" crept into my vocabulary, I should have known it wasn't right. Out of a fear of being looked down on for never having been in a relationship, I pushed through and ignored my feelings.

I felt innocent for my age and no longer wanted to feel young. Another really misinformed mindset. I felt like I was really immature, and a relationship would finally solve that problem... it didn't. I thought people would finally look at me differently. They didn't.

He was good to me, but it still didn't feel right. I was always crying because I didn't know what to do, so I just stuck it out and looked forward to when I would move away. When I didn't like something or didn't really care, I was a pretty transparent person, so I didn't know if he saw through this, but he eventually broke up with me.

I saw it coming and I had been crying a lot because I was so unhappy. I thought I was supposed to cry when we broke up, so that is what I did, but I didn't really feel like I had to. I cried because it did suck getting broken up with, and I felt like I should be sad. Instead, I felt a sense of freedom. When people broke up in movies, they were sad, so then why wasn't I?

Relationships aren't always as they seem, and "signs" are not the best deciding factors. I believe the signs we see in our lives are manipulated by the things we want to believe. I wanted to believe that I could be in a relationship, so I compromised everything and looked for things that would give me the okay, even though all odds in the universe were telling me otherwise.

This chapter is a reminder to live in the present and try your best to not make up stories. It was a major realization for me that those rom-coms every Friday were hurting me more than helping me. The tactics I used in the previous chapters helped me reconnect with reality and find myself again, along with cutting down the screen time for these movies and choosing to watch action and other genres instead.

You may know the feeling of embarrassment when you have made the wrong decision and now have to backtrack. You probably understand the pressure of growing up and 'experiencing life' as a teenager. The reality is that there is no typical teenage formula for life that you have to follow, but there are definitely stereotypes in the movies that try to normalize youthful and scandalous teenage behaviour. Maybe it would be helpful to think about the material you are feeding your brain and decide if this is beneficial to your mental health and well-being.

Is the media you're consuming helping you or hurting you?

Part 11: Becoming Me, Again

This is how I found my way through the dark forest of self-doubt and navigated the jungle of social pressure.

This is how I learned how to become me, again.

This is how I took back control of my life...

I Am in Control of My Life

I once heard that the standard of beauty is not actually made up out of thin air. Rather it has always been a reflection of social status. When I was growing up, a symbol of beauty was to be considered thin. I believe it was because being thin represented both self-restraint and having the time and money required to take care of your body. After looking at models over time, I noticed that standards of beauty changed throughout the ages, yet different body shapes always existed. Beautiful bodies are not determined by a magazine's photoshopped image but instead by the people within your community. If you notice that no one around you looks surreal it is because they are what natural human bodies look like.

As we go through our journey of life, we experience what I like to refer to as 'horribles'. We experience things like false hope, heartbreak, death, and bullying, and it would be so easy to use these excuses as reasons for not trying. The truth is, everyone has or will experience some version of what they might consider severe trauma in their lives. Horrible experiences are relative, and each experience is important in shaping who you are. Each time we experienced something awful, it was the universe presenting us with a choice that would determine who we became based on the choices we made in the moment.

I think most people become who they become as a result of making easier choices in the moment without thinking about the bigger picture of their life. These choices are often due to an unwillingness to take risks and a tendency to lead with their rational brain instead of their heart. By making the harder choices in the moment and anticipating a better future, people can choose who they become.

Everything is a choice if you choose to position it as one. People who make conscious choices to design their lives believe they are responsible for their wins and their failures, for their life experiences, and for their outputs into the world. We were born with the opportunity to make easy choices or hard choices, and who we become is the result of the choices we make.

Final Thoughts

These pages contain the thoughts I had and the lessons I have learned - in many cases, the hard way - throughout my adolescence. These lessons taught me many things and I hope they can help guide you through your own dark forest.

I have laid out the thoughts and lessons I learned growing up that have worked for me. I hope you feel less alone.

Everyone has different needs and thoughts, so not all of my strategies may work for you. The goal is to be your true self. I hope that my stories help you remember that you are not alone and support you on your journey to accept who you are and become who you want to be.

Here's to becoming you, again - to your hopes, to your dreams, and to reconnecting with your true authentic self.

Acknowledgements

Thank you to my family. I really appreciate your unconditional love and support while I was learning to love myself. I am so so soooo grateful for your ability to see through my bad moods and love me for the true authentic person I am and you knew I could be.

Thank you, Mom, for always being there for me and motivating me to keep writing. I admire you for your mental strength and perseverance.

Thank you, Dad, for encouraging me in all aspects of my school study and as my field hockey coach. You inspire me every day to be more and more clever so I am always one step, or ten steps ahead, to outwit you. And for driving me everywhere. Like EVERYwhere! (Including crazy!)

Thank you, Cameron, my brother, for inspiring me to be who I am today and teaching me so much about myself and others. Your drive and determination constantly motivate me to be a better version of myself.

Thank you to my Grandma, Rosalie (otherwise known as Super Cool Ninja Grandma), for supporting me no matter what and showing me what a truly positive attitude can be. Thank you to my Grandpa, Art, who passed away when I was 16, for being an unwavering role model of determination and dedication.

Thank you Auntie Carla for listening, supporting, and encouraging me to be the person I am today.

Thank you to my extended family, especially Uncle Chris, Auntie Suzie, Josée, Hugh, and Martin-Pierre. You've always shown genuine interest in my life and you are people who I know that I can count on.

Thank you to my friends who have shaped who I am today.

Thank you Lucy for helping me get through Chemistry and never failing to make me laugh during Choir. Thank you for making me feel heard and understood. I am so grateful for you, and you truly helped me become more positive and feel seen.

Thank you Adele for making my childhood so much fun and continuing to be there for me throughout high school and beyond. I have loved all our adventures including bike rides around Stanley Park and DQ runs!

Thank you Stella for encouraging me to believe in myself, raise my standards, and for uplifting me. Also thank you for letting me crash your family holidays and visit you!

Thank you to the girls on my field hockey teams who fostered a welcoming and encouraging environment.

Thank you Mr. O'Donnell for helping me to find my voice and encouraging me to be vulnerable. Thank you to Dr. Beukema for mentoring me and spending time with me to help me learn and grow as a person. Thank you to my teachers for helping me learn accountability, respect, and the feeling of achievement after hard work.

I want to acknowledge the mentors I had through reading: Alex Banayan, Seth Godin, Thomas Corley, Tony Robbins, James Clear, and Robin Sharma. Thank you, all, for writing books and creating media that encourages me to keep going.

Without a doubt, there are many people I have not mentioned here. Thank you to everyone who made my life better, either by supporting me or helping me learn a lesson!

Book Recommendations

The Four Agreements, by Don Miguel Ruiz

Atomic Habits, by James Clear

The Third Door, by Alex Banayan

In the Flo, by Alisa Vitti

The Monk Who Sold his Ferrari, by Robin Sharma

What To Do When It's Your Turn, by Seth Godin

Into The Magic Shop, by Dr. James Doty

The Alchemist, by Paulo Coelho

The Big Leap, by Gay Hendricks

The 5am Club, by Robin Sharma

Rich Habits, by Thomas Corley

Girl, Wash Your Face, by Rachel Hollis